THE BEAT FACE OF GOD:

The Beat Generation Writers as Spirit Guides

BY STEPHEN D. EDINGTON

To: Brian – Great to have you here – with appreciation for you interest in 'things Beat'

Stephen Edington

Big Sur, CA

With A Foreword By

DAVID AMRAM

January 15, 2006

First Edition
Editor: Nita Van Zandt
Front cover: Designed by Richard Widhu as a visual representation of Allen
Ginsberg's *Sunflower Sutra*.

Stephen D. Edington
9 Vespa Lane
Nashua, New Hampshire 03064

Note for Librarians: A cataloguing record for this book is available from Library and
Archives Canada at www.collectionscanada.ca/amicus/index-e.html
ISBN 1-4120-5374-9

Printed in Victoria, BC, Canada. Printed on paper with minimum 30% recycled fibre.
Trafford's print shop runs on "green energy" from solar, wind and other environmentally-
friendly power sources.

Offices in Canada, USA, Ireland and UK
This book was published on-demand in cooperation with Trafford Publishing. On-demand
publishing is a unique process and service of making a book available for retail sale to the
public taking advantage of on-demand manufacturing and Internet marketing. On-demand
publishing includes promotions, retail sales, manufacturing, order fulfilment, accounting and
collecting royalties on behalf of the author.

Book sales for North America and international:
Trafford Publishing, 6E–2333 Government St.,
Victoria, BC v8T 4P4 CANADA
phone 250 383 6864 (toll-free 1 888 232 4444)
fax 250 383 6804; email to orders@trafford.com
Book sales in Europe:
Trafford Publishing (UK) Ltd., Enterprise House, Wistaston Road Business Centre,
Wistaston Road, Crewe, Cheshire CW2 7RP UNITED KINGDOM
phone 01270 251 396 (local rate 0845 230 9601)
facsimile 01270 254 983; orders.uk@trafford.com
Order online at:
trafford.com/05-0269

10 9 8 7 6

DEDICATED TO THE MEMORIES OF:

Lucien Carr

Philip Lamantia

Robert Creeley

Hunter S. Thompson

They moved to the other side of the curtain while I wrote this book.

May they rest in beatific peace.

to be yourself in a world that is doing its best, day and night, to ask you to be like everybody else—is to fight the hardest battle any human being can fight.

e.e. cummings

THE BEAT FACE OF GOD

Permissions

Acknowledgements

Writing a book is a daunting task. One of the rewards of taking on such a task, however, is the acquaintances and friendships that are made, and the existing ones that are deepened, as the writing process goes forward. I think of this now as I consider all the wonderful people I wish to thank for their role in helping me produce this book.

To begin, literally, at the beginning, I thank Richard Widhu, a very artistically gifted member of my congregation for designing the front cover.

David Amram has been a dear friend for a number of years. I'm grateful for the unrelenting encouragement and good will he's shown me as I prepared this work; and I'm especially grateful for his kind and generous words in the Foreword.

Maura Shaw is an editor for publishing company in Vermont. She gave me the idea for this book in the first place and helped me in its early stages. Thanks, Maura.

As was the case with my book *Kerouac's Nashua Connection*, Nita Van Zandt has proved to be a most capable Editor—for which I thank her once again. Anya Zakiewicz helped with proof reading. Rose Edington and Melvin Hoover were of great help to me when it came to a final going over of the text, as was Douglas Stevenson. Thanks to all of you.

When my friend Jerry Cimino read an early draft of what was then an embryonic work in progress he wrote to say, "Steve, you've got to write this book!" OK, I did. Jerry operates the Beat Museum in Monterey, California—when, that is, he's not on the road himself spreading the gospel of the Beats with his Beatmobile. Thanks for your support, Jerry, and keep up the good work.

John Cassady has been a supportive friend through all of this, and I'm especially grateful to him for the insights he's given me into his father, Neal. Carolyn Cassady has been a great help in bringing me to a clearer understanding of Neal Cassady, and in helping me out with the Neal chapter. John and Carolyn—thanks to you both.

Al Hinkle shared some wonderful Neal stories with me; and his daughter, Dawn Davis, offered some good information on the life of Neal Cassady as well, for which I thank them. In addition, I thank them for being delightful people who are just plain fun to be around.

Leon Tabory and Ann Marie (Murphy) Maxwell have also shared their recollections of Neal Cassady with me over the years. I thank them each for their helpful insights.

Nancy Peters at City Light Books in San Francisco has been a source of encouragement and support, for which I thank her.

Another Nancy from the West Coast I must thank is Nancy Lewis, owner and operator of Red Hot Promotions of Sausalito, California. She took an interest in my work early on, and has encouraged me along the way.

I thank Dennis McNally, author of *Desolate Angel: Jack Kerouac, The Beat Generation, and America* and *A Long Strange Trip—The Inside History of the Grateful Dead* for his personal support and encouragement.

George Wallace, of Huntington, New York, is yet another of my Beat-aficionado friends who has helped me to keep on keeping on with a work like this. Thanks, George.

I thank Professor Hilary Holladay at the University of Massachusetts at Lowell, for her interest in my work, and for her support and encouragement.

John Sampas of Lowell, Massachusetts, has also been most supportive, for which I thank him.

I'm sure my interest in the Beats would not have gotten to the point where it is had it not been for my involvement with the Lowell Celebrates Kerouac! Committee for the past fifteen years. Through this Committee I first met Paul Marion, who has remained a good friend and has cheered me on in my writing. Among the current LCK Committee members to whom I feel a special indebtedness for both keeping the Kerouac flame alive, and keeping me going in my own Beat explorations, are Lawrence Carradini (President), Margaret Smith, Richard Hyatt, Philip Chaput, and Nancy Herbstman.

THE BEAT FACE OF GOD

I cannot conclude this without also thanking the members of the Unitarian Universalist Church of Nashua, New Hampshire—my wonderful congregation—for indulging me in my interests of all things Beat. I just hope I don't over-do it too much in my sermons.

Finally—as was the case with my previous book—I thank my wife, Michele, and our son, Gordon, for once again putting up with my obsession. I'll try to cool it for awhile now.

Stephen D. Edington
Nashua, New Hampshire

THE BEAT FACE OF GOD: THE BEAT GENERATION WRITERS AS SPIRIT GUIDES

Table Of Contents

Author's Preface

In a review of a recently released collection of previously unpublished journal writings by Jack Kerouac [*Windblown World: The Journals of Jack Kerouac, 1947-1954*. Douglas Brinkley, Editor. Viking, 2004] Walter Kirn, writing for the The New York Times, quipped that this particular release "may at first strike readers as an attempt to squeeze yet more toothpaste out of Kerouac's flattened tube." That seemingly dismissive remark notwithstanding, Mr. Kirn went on to write a largely favorable review of the book.

Kirn's remark, however, might also well apply to yet another book being written about the Beats—like, say, this one. Has the Beat Renaissance, which began in earnest towards the latter part of 1980s, become a flattened tube from which very little toothpaste can now be extracted? I'm not convinced of that; and I'm certainly not convinced that this work of mine represents the last squeeze, as it were.

But, while granting that the focus of this book is largely on the lives of some of the Beat Generation writers and their works, I do not regard it primarily as a Beat Book as such. It is a book about spirituality, and a personal exploration of the impact Beat writing has had on me. It is written for anyone who is pursuing a spiritual path whether he or she is all that familiar with the Beats or not.

The Beat Face of God represents my attempt to bring together two of the worlds in which I live and move: the world of a minister and religious leader; and the world of a Beat Generation aficianado and scholar. I use the word scholar with trepidation. In the Beat/Kerouac world, through which I've circulated for nearly two decades now, I've come to know many people—some of whom have become good friends—whose knowledge of all things Beat far exceeds my own. But I think I can offer a perspective on the Beats that will speak to both of these worlds.

I am a religious leader whose personal spiritual journey has been been greatly influenced by the lives and writings of a loose confederation of writers and poets who came into their own in America in the aftermath of the Second World War and beyond This was a time when I was still in my childhood. My spiritual wellsprings are fed by them; and some of my most enjoyable moments are spent in the company of those who also delight in recalling and celebrating the works, and the legacies, of those from that era. In the writings of the Beats I also find a way of maintaining my sanity, and preserving a measure of hope, in a land that is becoming increasingly devoid of each. I address this matter in my concluding chapter.

So I'm really not trying to add to the pile of some of the truly outstanding, and scholarly, work that has been done on the lives, the writings, and the legacies of the Beats. I draw on some of that work, along with my personal encounters with these remarkable folk, in an attempt to make the Beats accessible to a wider range of persons than those who are presently attracted to them. My work and calling as a minister, in a liberal Protestant (or post-Protestant) denomination, the Unitarian Universalist Association, continually makes me aware of the spiritual yearnings that persist—perhaps more strongly than ever—in modern, and post-modern society. The greatest, and still most uncharted area of our personal and shared existence, as human beings, remains that of inner space.

This yearning for spiritual depth can take persons in a variety of directions, some more healthy than others. It can ally one with some of the more reactive, and reactionary, forces in both American, and global, society. It can render one vulnerable to all manner of manipulation and exploitation. But the spiritual drive itself is real, and is one of the more crucial and authentic dimensions of our humanity. We all search, and reach, both within ourselves and beyond ourselves for meaning, purpose, and depth in living. We often do so in the face of a culture that celebrates banality, inanity, and mindless consumption for its own sake.

In the Beats I see spiritual rebels, or holy mis-fits as I like to call them. They, too, had their share of banality and inanity to deal with. But rather than slouch into nihilism or despair, they chose to celebrate the Life Force instead.

They cultivated a spirituality, in a variety of ways, that sought an enlightened and humanistic present—as well as one that looked towards an enlightened and humanistic future—rather than one that catered to the forces of reaction. Some of them, tragically, got too close to the Torch of Life, and flamed out; but others remained—and some still remain—warmed by that Torch throughout their lives. For those who still seek that Life Force, and who long for the warmth and nurture of the Torch of Life, the Beats—those who are still alive and those who have passed on—remain available. I hope to make that availability better known in the pages ahead.

You're invited to a journey here. Along the way remember to practice kindness, to do good where you can, and to heed your own beat—even as you take a cue or two from the Beats themselves.

Rev. Steve Edington

Nashua, New Hampshire

March, 2005

Foreword

By
David Amram

Steve Edington's *The Beat Face of God* is a welcome addition to the ever-growing series of books that are being written about what is called the Beat Generation. Almost all of us who were a part of this experience came to reject the whole "Beat" stereotype, which became part of the cultural vocabulary following the phenomenal success of the publication in 1957 of Jack Kerouac's *On the Road*. Suddenly "Beat" became an instant slogan. Kerouac became an appointed leader of a cultural explosion, and an overnight movement was officially born. But much of this explosion degraded Jack's classic book, and came to misrepresent the values that he and I and all of us espoused.

On the Road, one of Jack's many wonderful books, was in part a report of the work we were all trying to do, as well as a documentation of the egalitarian friendships we formed and the openheartedness of those friendships. It was also about the many forms of spirituality we celebrated in our everyday struggles as we tried to survive and celebrate life in the highly repressive atmosphere of a new conformist America that replaced the euphoria of the immediate post World War II days.

But Beat became a flavor of the month, rather than a philosophy or an inquiry into life. The fashion industry, the entertainment industry and TV (we didn't call it The Media way back then) all latched on to what was bring presented as the latest fad, more akin to the hula hoop or the padded bra rather than anything relating to new artistic values or new ways of understanding a changing society. We were a new generation of artists of all disciplines, all of whom shared fresh values and a new way of informing others about a desire for positive change. So, the last thing that anyone ever thought about when hearing of these new crazy people, who were supposed to be Beat, was that Beat was also a deeply spiritual way of approaching life. No one ever equated art in the America of the 1950s with anything to do with any kind of religious experience.

Jews, Muslims, Buddhists and all people who practiced other ways of worship, including the timeless beliefs of our Native Americans, were considered complete outsiders. The consensus was that their religious practices should remain invisible or be the sole province of anthropologists, or of background cast members of Hollywood costume movies about primitives of ancient times. Practitioners of any kind of alternative faith or approach to the spiritual life were considered sacrilegious un-Americans who were to be ignored for advocating such beliefs which proved that they were delusional crackpots and sinners.

There was one positive side to all this, however, in that during the 1950s we were spared the current plethora of gurus with limos, Bible thumping televangelists, and New Age rip-off artists blaspheming the sacred religions of the East. They hadn't yet become businesses and rapid growth industries that exploited the commercial values of how one could worship the mysteries of life by charging exorbitant fees to others to find out these secrets. That all started in the 1960s.

The spiritual path for us was, as it has always been throughout history, a simple as well as a natural one for those interested in a deeper understanding of life itself. Most of us had been brought up in a family setting where our religious identity was given to us at an early age. Even though Jack Kerouac admired Buddhism, and had a great knowledge of it, he remained a devout Catholic. I remember him taking me to my first Mass, and how we spent countless late nights and early morning hours discussing the values of many religious traditions, including my Jewish heritage. We also discussed the relationship of all major religions, each of which we felt was an important way of better understanding who we were and why we are here.

Gary Snyder and Philip Whalen were both true scholarly Buddhists, and Allen Ginsberg, while raised Jewish, embraced many different faiths. Gregory Corso, like his fellow poets Philip Lamantia and Howard Hart, remained Catholic, and often took me to a Catholic Church in Greenwich Village, where he was baptized. This was where he also requested his memorial service be held when he passed away. Patti Smith and I played at that service. Neal Cassady retained his Catholic roots even though he was an expert on the teachings of Edgar Cayce. I have always maintained and celebrated my Jewish upbringing.

Charlie Parker, Dizzy Gillespie, Theolonious Monk and countless other giants of jazz I was blessed to know and play with, always stressed the importance of preaching when you play, and of the deep roots of church in all their music. They knew that music, above all else, was a spiritual force that could bring the world together.

The importance of touching one's spiritual roots and heritage was impressed upon both Jack Kerouac and me by some of the women we knew. This was especially true with the artist and Native American painter Dody Mueller. Jack and I shared a lifelong interest and respect for Native American traditions; and it was Dody who told Jack that he should search for his own French Canadian—Indian connection, even as she had explored her own Native American background. Dody told Jack this was a trail he had to walk alone, just as she had done.

The variety of beliefs and how they were practiced and shared by the often wild and eccentric members of our ad hoc group reflects the variety and unpredictable nature of all who were involved. They also recount the variety of ways that the spiritual side of life was so vital to us all. If we had one thing in common, though, there in the 1950s, it was that none of us were looking for a quick-fix, thirty second solution on how to achieve Nirvana. Jack himself had said that Beat meant Beatific, i.e. living a day to day life in accordance with the Beatitudes of Jesus and the Teachings of the Buddha. In this respect it is fitting that his grave marker bears the words, "He honored life." This is what we were all, each in our own way, trying to do.

Steve Edington's important new book, *The Beat Face of God*, shares the importance of this element of spirituality in our era, and how we celebrated it. Rev. Edington is not only a well respected minister. He is also one of the first scholars to do thorough research on the subject of Kerouac's family roots in Nashua, New Hampshire—where he has been, since 1988, the minister of the Unitarian Unversalist Church. He has also been one of the central figures in the annual Lowell Celebrates Kerouac Festival, considered by many to be the premier event of this kind.

Edington is not a guru with a limo, or a hustler of misinformation guaranteed to gain you Enlightenment. This book has no CD-ROM attached, merchandising T-shirts, fake religious items, organizations to join, or secret society handshakes. Neither does it come with a warranty that promises immortality with only fifteen minutes a day of practice, if you become Rev. Edington's follower for life. What he offers instead is a book that is down to earth, warm, informative, and chock full of information. It is well researched and written in a style that is so clear and enjoyable that even the most hard core atheist will join those who practice some form of spiritual celebration in savoring the wealth of this important new work.

In thinking back to the era of which Edington writes, I'm aware that we were not what one would call a Movement with a unified party line of any kind. But we *were* true believers in the sanctity of life and the miracle of being here, knowing that there was a Greater Power somewhere. We also knew that no matter how crazy things got it was of the utmost importance to remember to honor each and every person on Earth. This form of spirituality has been common to almost every tribal culture that has ever survived for any length of time, since the beginning of time. None of us felt that the spiritual part of life was anything other than a natural reflection of how to look at things as they really were, to try to understand why we are here, and to do what we could and should to honor that Higher Power. We knew that there were greater forces in this world and universe than we could ever fully understand, and that any form of creativity was a form of worship.

Thanks to Steve Edington we now have a book that tells us about all of this. It tells of how spirituality was a central part of our lives during an amazing time, and among an amazing group of people—many of whom have left us work of enduring value. The fact that so many of us found one another, haphazardly criss-crossing paths as kindred spirits, was a miracle in itself. It also produced some miraculous results, many of which Edington has written about. Like the finest of sermons, reading *The Beat Face of God* is an energizing and inspiring experience, giving hope and positive feelings to the reader.

In my faith there is a famous prayer which asks the question, "How can we sing the Lord's song in a strange land?" This was a question we all asked ourselves most of our lives, years before we all met. Steve Edington's book shares some answers to this age old question, by documenting how so many of us tried to find our own way and sing our own songs. This is a book that all generations can share as a family with one another.

Mel Brooks, in his 1960 classic *The 2000 Year Old Man*, said, "You raise my hopes and lift my spirits." We can all say the same thing today as a way of thanking Steve Edington for his gift to us all.

David Amram
Putnam Valley, New York
March, 2005

CHAPTER ONE

They Were Seeking a Gospel

W ho *were* those guys? And for the most part, yes, they were guys. When they first surfaced into view in the late 1950s the pop-culture label that got attached to them was "beatnik." But that was not a label they chose for themselves. The late Herb Caen, a very popular and witty columnist for the *San Francisco Chronicle,* came up with that word; and he largely intended it as a put-down of what passed for an American counter-culture in the 50s. Beatniks, in the popular mind of that time, were shiftless ne'er-do-wells who sported scrawny goatees, wrote bad poetry, lived in unkempt "pads" with their "chicks," and eschewed honest work. Their popular prototype was the character of Maynard G. Krebs, as played by Bob Denver, on the television show *The Many Loves of Dobie Gillis.* Maynard, however, was a benign, cleaned-up, made-for-TV beatnik who was suitable for family viewing. His abhorrence to work was more tailored for the laugh track than anything else. In my early teens—which came in the late 1950s—I can recall a run of years when dressing up as a beatnik was a popular Halloween costume which was guaranteed to get a few chuckles as you went trick-or-treating.

But these beatniks were also seen as having something of a sinister aura about them. In the mainstream American mind they posed a vague and largely undefined threat to all that was right and good about the country and the culture. Part of that perceived threat was rooted in the fear that each adult generation has of its coming-of-age younger generation, but with the Beats it ran deeper than that. Indeed, in a speech given before the 1960

Republican National Convention, FBI Director J. Edgar Hoover sounded an alert to the nation when he stated that the three major enemies of America were "Communists, eggheads, and beatniks." Who *were* those guys? How did they manage to evoke both the ridicule of the self-appointed keepers of the culture of their day, as well as the wrath and loathing of America's chief law enforcement officer?

The term "Beat Generation" itself was actually coined some 12 years before Mr. Hoover launched his beatnik jeremiad. The story, which is now a part of the Beat lore, is that there were two young, aspiring, and still unpublished writers, who had a conversation in a New York City apartment in the summer of 1948. They were trying to come up with a name or phrase that would capture the mood and characterize the spiritual challenge of their generation—the generation coming of age either during or immediately after the Second World War. The term Lost Generation, used to describe the mood of cynicism and disillusionment of the post World War I generation, no longer seemed to fit. As they rolled the issue around one of them said, "I guess we're a beat generation." It clicked. The two decided they'd hit the right note.

The two young men were Jack—originally named Jean Louis—Kerouac and John Clellon Holmes. Kerouac had come to New York in 1940 from the French-Canadian Catholic working class neighborhoods of Lowell, Massachusetts on the strength of a football scholarship to Columbia University. He first had to spend a preparatory year at the Horace Mann School in New York before entering Columbia in the fall of 1941. By 1948 he'd long dropped out of Columbia and had made two seagoing runs as a member of the U.S. Merchant Marine during World War II.

Holmes was from a WASPy family in Old Saybrook, Connecticut and had served in the Hospital Corps of the United States Navy before following his literary dreams to New York City. Both of these gentlemen knew that they were not cut out for the emerging corporate culture of post-World War II America, and they were each trying to help the other find their respective poetic and literary voices.

Four years prior to this celebrated conversation Kerouac had met up with Allen Ginsberg and William S. Burroughs in and around the environs of Columbia University. The three of them, along with various others, formed a literary camaraderie within which they shared their fledgling writing endeavors. They also engaged in extended discussions at their favorite urban haunts about the overall direction of the culture in which they had come to early adulthood, and what they might have to say about it. Holmes did not come into this circle until 1948, and he felt a kinship with these folk on the one hand while keeping something of a philosophical distance from them on the other.

In time, both Holmes and Kerouac would publish their signature novels—*Go* for Holmes in 1950, and *On the Road* for Kerouac in 1957. Each of these books, in its own way, fleshed out the mood the two writers were struggling to identify in their 1948 conversation. As the term Beat gained currency, and then later become debased as beatnik, these two continued to insist that they and their fellow Beats were really pilgrims on a religious and spiritual quest in the new and uncertain land that America had become following the most devastating war in human history.

In the larger society, however, the persons identifying themselves as part of the Beat Generation of the late 1940s and 1950s appeared to be the very antithesis of the religious and spiritual ethos of the immediate post World War II years in America. To think of religion and spirituality in the America of the 1950s is to think of Billy Graham crusades or the early television broadcasts of Bishop Fulton J. Sheen. It is to recall the construction boom of mainline Protestant churches in America's newly emerging suburbs. It is to remember President Eisenhower opening his 1953 Inaugural Address by asking the nation to join him in a word of prayer. To disavow or ignore traditional religion, as it was conventionally understood then, was to place oneself under suspicion of not quite being a real and true American. When, in 1954, the United States Congress, by Official Act, added the words "under God" to the Pledge of Allegiance to the American flag it was reflecting and validating this cultural ethos. In taking this action, the 1954 Congress was also, in effect, equating atheism with anti-Americanism.

Unlike the 1960s, there was precious little that passed for a counterculture in the America of the 1950s. The Beats probably came the closest, although Hettie (Cohen) Jones, the one-time wife of LeRoi Jones (now Amiri Baraka), probably wasn't too far off the mark when she wryly observed that the entire Beat Generation population could have fit into the living room of her and Roi's small New York City apartment in the early 1950s. And if religion, in the popular mind of that day, was associated with such traits as order, piety, conformity, and obedience to authority, then the Beats were truly an affront to any and all things religious and spiritual.

But, as just noted, the two individuals who are generally credited with coining the name Beat Generation spoke of it in clearly religious terms. What Kerouac and Holmes had both recognized as they were having that Beat Generation conversation, was a kind of uneasiness and furtiveness among the persons of their age. These people still had most of their lives in front of them, and were wondering and asking "What's next?" following the most devastating war that human beings had ever waged.

To be Beat, as Holmes and Kerouac saw it, was to be reduced to one's essentials. It was to have all pretexts, poses, and pretensions stripped away and to find oneself facing such bare-naked questions as, "Who am I?" and "How do I make some sense of my life as well as Life Itself?" These questions had taken on a new kind of relevancy in a world that had just witnessed death on a level never before known in human history; and had seen the expendability, and disposability, of human life demonstrated in ways never seen before.

These are ongoing and universal questions, however. They pose themselves, at one time or another, to practically any person who has any kind of capacity for self-reflection, regardless of the historical setting in which they arise. Sometimes when I'm walking alone on a city street with no urgent appointment or task, I will get a light and lost sensation that "it's just me out here." At such moments I don't quite know where to go, or why I should keep walking along that particular street. I call these my Beat Moments. For me these moments bring to mind the words of a familiar African-American spiritual: "It's not my brother or my sister but it's me O Lord, standin' in the need of prayer." While I don't address prayers to a listening Deity myself, I am nonetheless aware in moments like these that I am reaching beyond myself for some kind of meaning and some kind of blessing without specifically knowing what, or who, it is I'm reaching for. It is at times like these that I feel a spiritual connection to many of the Beats, who were also reaching beyond themselves without quite knowing what their hands would touch.

The term Beat, however, was hardly confined to any one expression or mood. Another understanding of Beat was that it meant being beaten down or beaten out to the fringes of the mainstream culture. To be Beat was to know that you were a mis-fit in the most literal sense of the word. It was to have the soul-level knowledge that you didn't quite fit in, that you didn't quite belong. This was how many of the Beats felt when it came to the direction America in the 1950s was taking as it craved normalcy once again after a terrible war that had been preceded by a crippling economic Depression.

One person who especially epitomized this dimension of Beat was a Times Square denizen named Herbert Huncke. Huncke was a petty thief, low-level drug dealer, and con-man. He was also of middle class origins, a well-read person of great intelligence, a quick wit, a raconteur, and an all-round charmer. Herbert Huncke was someone who had deliberately chosen to not "go along." He was getting by solely on his own wits and on his own terms. Huncke's use of the term Beat came from the down-and-out streets where beat meant being completely worn down, and with no one but yourself and your hustle, or your con-job skills, to rely on. As Huncke himself would explain many decades later near the end of his life, "When I said I was beat man, I mean I was beat!"

Very few of the Beats actually emulated Huncke's day-to-day life-style, however, and some of them even got burned by his hustles and con-jobs on occasion. But they were quite taken with his overall style and attitude nonetheless. In their eyes Huncke was the ultimate outsider. When Kerouac suggested the name Beat Generation to Holmes, he at least in part had Herb Huncke in mind.

Four years after his conversation with Kerouac, John Holmes wrote an article for the November 16, 1952 issue of *The New York Times Magazine* titled *This is the Beat Generation.* In it he wrote, "Unlike the Lost Generation, which was more occupied with the loss of faith, the Beat Generation is becoming more and more occupied with the need for it." Following the publication of his signature novel, *On the Road,* Jack Kerouac would assert that "The Beat Generation is a religious generation." Shortly after the Holmes article appeared, Kerouac would link the term Beat with Beatitude, saying that to be Beat was to show simple kindness, compassion, and sympathy in a culture that demonstrated very little sympathy for those who were not attuned to its general ethos and values. Kerouac drew on the beatitudes, as put forth by Jesus of Nazareth in the Sermon on the Mount, for this explanation of what it meant to be Beat. For Kerouac, Beat also implied a kind of sadness, a sense of the life's tragic dimension, and of the need to find joy in the face of sadness and tragedy.

So how, then, do we go about understanding the Beat Generation as a religious movement, and some of the literature it produced as being spiritual guideposts? Let's start with this: One of my colleagues in the Unitarian Universalist ministry, the Rev. Forrest Church, has defined religion as: "Our human response to the dual reality of being alive and knowing that we will die." Other definitions of religion could be offered, but this is an especially good one, I feel. Rev. Church's definition of religion also states what the spiritual quest is really all about. To be on a spiritual path is to be discovering how to respond to life, how to choose life, how to say yes to life even as we know our earthly lives are not ours forever. How to truly embrace life in the face of death is the spiritual challenge, both in this age and in all previous human eras. Spirituality is also about the pursuit of Relationship with a capital 'R'. It is to seek a connection with a Larger Reality (by whatever name one chooses to call it) that enfolds us all and transcends the atomistic self.

Drawing on these understandings of religion and spirituality then, Kerouac was also dead on the mark in calling the Beat Generation a religious generation. Journalist and historian David Halberstam gave the movement a succinct, but accurate, summation when he looked back on that time from the perspective of the 1990s, and noted that the Beats were writers, artists, and poets who were "seeking spiritual destinies."

As noted, the original Beats wrote against the backdrop of a world that had witnessed death on a scale never before seen. There were battlefield deaths, the deaths of civilian populations across Europe, the systematized and assembly-line deaths of the Holocaust, and the mega-death and destruction brought on by the atomic bombs dropped on Hiroshima and Nagasaki. This horror was all shortly followed by the almost incomprehensible revelations of the death industry of Joseph Stalin's pre- and post-War Soviet Union. With this kind of death laden back-drop, the real religious and spiritual challenge of the 1950s was how meaningfully live after a time in which life had been made to look very cheap.

But the mainstream American response to this challenge, by and large, was to place a veneer of normality and conformity over the fears, disruptions, and hunger for meaning that the Second World War generated. The cultural imperative was to get back to normal. In some ways this was quite understandable since the country had endured some 15 years of disruption and uncertainty brought on first by the Depression and then the War. We had just been through the most horrifying chapter in human history; albeit with America being spared an up close and personal exposure to that horror. (The Americans who fought in WWII are the obvious exception to this.) So following, first, a Depression and then a mega-war, the cultural mood and longing were for a time, and for a state of mind, in which "everything is alright now." It was time to settle down, find one's niche, and fly right.

In response to this cultural mood, William Levitt started building the first suburb in the potato fields of New York's Long Island. The GI Bill, one of the more remarkable and far reaching pieces of legislation ever enacted by the United States Congress, sent thousands of returning GIs to the campuses of America's colleges and universities. According these highly deserving war veterans the benefits of a college education was clearly laudable. One by-product of the GI bill, for better or for worse though, was that many of its recipients were groomed and trained for the roles they would play in the emerging collective corporate culture of post-War America. And hovering over all of this was the religious revival of the 1950s, placing a kind of Divine sanction over this emerging "American way of life."

But everything wasn't alright. The grade school classes I attended in the early 50s were occasionally interrupted by Duck and Cover air raid drills. We little kids had to go out into the hallway, get down on our knees, and curl into little balls against the wall, thereby learning how to protect ourselves just in case the Russians (whoever they were) would drop something called the atomic bomb on us. There were also these evil entities out there somewhere—it wasn't altogether clear in my young mind if they were even people—called Communists, who vaguely had something to do with these bombs that might get dropped on us. We were always supposed to be keeping an eye out for the Communists, even if we didn't know what they looked like or what they did. Among the first radio broadcasts I can remember listening to were the Joseph McCarthy hearings, and I found it very scary indeed to hear that these Communists were actually right here in my very own America.

What we had then was a cultural overlay of "everything is alright if we'll just fly right" serving as a veneer for an undercurrent of fear, uncertainty, emptiness, and spiritual vacuousness. In my case, to tell the truth, the veneer worked pretty well. In grade school I learned to protect myself from Russian bombs; but at the end of the week I could still go to Sunday School and be reassured that "Jesus loves me this I know, for the Bible tells me so." While it was never stated in so many words I nonetheless had the sense that Jesus was somehow an American—or at least he clearly would have been had my country been around in his day.

Be all that as it may, beneath that veneer of normalcy and conformity was a restlessness and an edginess and a largely undefined thirst for life that would not settle down, much less fly right. This spiritual restlessness gave birth to the Beats. As the reader has probably already figured out I was too young to catch the first wave of such restlessness. Like Anne Waldman, the author of *The Beat Book*, I like to call myself a second generation Beat. But in his book *Go*, the original Beat novel published in 1950, John Holmes captures this post World War II mood as he writes of a fictitious—but still very real—New York City jazz club called The Go Hole:

> These restless youngsters (were) finding a passion in this music [jazz] that belonged defiantly to them...The Go Hole was where all the high school bands, the swing bands, and the roadhouses of their lives had led these young people; and above it all was their vision of a wartime America as a monstrous dance land...In this modern jazz they heard something rebel and nameless and their lives knew a gospel for the first time. It was more than a music; it became an attitude toward life...and these introverted kids (emotional outcasts of a war they had been too young to join, or in which they had lost their innocence), who had never belonged anywhere before, now felt somewhere at last.

"Their lives knew a gospel for the first time..." That was an interesting choice of words on Holmes part. His restless kids are looking for a gospel. When Holmes wrote of how the Beat Generation was occupied with a "need for faith" he meant they were looking for something to believe in at a time when faith options seemed slim. And if the jazz musicians provided the music of this gospel, then the Beats were the gospel writers. If the role of 1950's mainstream religion with its traditional gospel was to maintain the veneer of normalcy, it was the Beats who were pushing and probing beneath the veneer. While Hettie Jones was probably right when she said that the writers, artists, and poets whose work and creativity were coming out of a Beat consciousness would have fit in her living room, there was a much larger consciousness they tapped into that was largely hidden in living rooms, bedrooms, classrooms, and basements across America.

I first discovered, via Jack Kerouac, the Beats in the late 1960s, just at the time when their day in the sun was being eclipsed by the Hippies. My own interest in the Beat era waned a bit in the 1980s until, in the summer of 1988 my family and I moved to Nashua, New Hampshire where I am the minister of the Unitarian Universalist Church. About this time that a Beat revival got underway. In that same summer of 1988 the Jack Kerouac Commemorative was dedicated in Lowell, Massachusetts, a city about 15 miles south of Nashua. Out of the successful effort to build the Kerouac Commemorative came the formation of the Lowell Celebrates Kerouac Committee which puts on an annual Kerouac Festival in early October. Over the years hundreds of people come from all parts of America, Canada, and from other countries around the world to attend and take part in this week-end event. A few years after my arrival in Nashua I joined this Committee, and have remained an active member ever since. Since 1997 the English Department at the University of Massachusetts at Lowell has sponsored a biennial Jack Kerouac Beat Literature Symposium that attracts Kerouac and Beat scholars from around the country.

In 1998 I was invited to teach a course at the University of Massachusetts at Lowell on "The Literature of the Beat Movement" which I continue to do. In 1999 I published the book *Kerouac's Nashua Connection*, which describes Kerouac's French-Canadian Catholic ancestry and how that ancestry has affected his writing. So, even as the Beats are having their revival, something that began for me clear back in the late 1960s has profoundly revived my own life over the past decade and more.

In the chapters that follow it is my intent to treat—drawing on both their lives and their writings—the Beat Generation writers as the authors of the gospel of an alternative spirituality and alternative religion of the 1950s. It is *not* my intent, however, to offer this as simply a piece of history. While I am not a professional historian, I believe the purpose of history is to inform and illuminate the age in which it is studied. For reasons I continue to try to grasp, the Beats are bigger now, in the early years of this new millennium, than they ever were in their supposed heyday of a half-century ago.

Most of my students in the Beat Literature course I teach are in their late 20s or 30s and are taking night classes in order to complete a degree. With just a few exceptions, they were nowhere close to even being born during the original Beat era. They have jobs and families. Many of them are in the process of finding their niche in the confused America of today. Hardly any of them are English majors. Many simply need an English course to round out their degree requirements, and mine just happens to fit their schedules. And yet I have seen the lives and works of the Beats connect with their lives often enough to know that the past is still very much present. Perhaps these folk, too, are seeking a gospel as they come of age in this land.

Serving on the Lowell Celebrates Kerouac Committee has also been a very interesting experience. Each year we put on a week-end long Kerouac festival in early October. I continue to be amazed at the people who come to Lowell each year to walk through the neighborhoods Kerouac writes about in many of his novels, and to visit his grave. They come as seekers on a holy pilgrimage, feeling that there is something in Jack Kerouac's life and writings that affects their lives.

My holy pilgrimage goes on as well. I too continue to seek, like those "restless youngsters" John Holmes described, and like those who come to Kerouac's grave, a gospel for myself. It was shortly before I entered theological school in the late 1960s that the poet, song-writer, and singer Paul Simon wrote *The Sounds of Silence.* One of the song's more haunting phrases makes reference to prophetic words being written on "subway walls" and on "tenement halls." This song has stayed with me over the ensuing decades since it was written. Whether or not Mr. Simon specifically had the Beats in mind when he wrote it, I don't know; but I make the metaphorical connection to them nonetheless.

Who *were* those guys? They were young men, and—yes—women, who demonstrated a very uncommon kind of courage. They dared to row, and write, against the societal tide of their youth. Some of them tragically succumbed to lives of self-destruction. Kerouac's alcoholism prevented him from even reaching his fiftieth birthday. Neal Cassady died alone of exhaustion alongside a stretch of railroad tracks in Mexico at age 42. Lew Welch took his life in a California desert at age 54.

Others, like Allen Ginsberg, lived to see their work gain acclaim and renown. In 1986 he was named Distinguished Professor at Brooklyn College. William Burroughs, who died within a few months of Ginsberg in 1997, was inducted into the American Academy and Institute of Arts and Letters in 1982. Some are still alive and well and fighting the good fight. Gary Snyder has retired from the English faculty at the University of California at Davis and continues his efforts of environmental advocacy. Lawrence Ferlinghetti is a former Poet Laureate of San Francisco and still owns the same City Lights Bookstore he purchased and opened in 1953. David Amram keeps proclaiming the Beat gospel, and keeps the Beat flame burning, with his tireless energy and his outstanding musical talent.

This Beat began in America's subterranean strata of the 1950s. It was from here that the Beats first offered up their gospel. Gospel, literally interpreted, means good news. What good news might these blessed and holy spiritual misfits of their day have to offer us in our day? This is what we shall continue to explore.

CHAPTER TWO

The Beat Generation Writers: My Spirit Guides

On a visit to the People's Republic of China in 1984 Allen Ginsberg composed a poem he called *Improvisation in Beijing*. The opening line states: "I write poetry because the English word Inspiration comes from Latin *Spiritus*, breath, I want to breathe freely." I'm not a poet but I read poetry and prose for the same reason; I, too, wish to breathe freely. *Spiritus*, breath. The spiritual quest is the quest to breathe; to breathe not just the breath of physical life, but the breath of what Jesus called The Life Abundant.

No one else, of course, can do your breathing for you, be it physical or spiritual. But there are people who on occasion come into our lives and who, so to speak, open up our lungs. They clear out our passages in order that *Spiritus* may enter our souls. Some of these people we may meet in the flesh and even come to know personally; others we encounter through their writings and sayings, their works of art, or by the tales told of their deeds and actions. However the meeting may take place, such men and women are our Spirit Guides. They open up our minds and hearts and souls in order that *Spiritus* may come in. Some of the great Spirit Guides of Humanity have had major religions emerge in their wake and in their name, whether they intended it or not: Moses, Jesus, Buddha, Mohammed, to cite some of the better known ones. Other Spirit Guides have touched lives on a much more limited scale, but their impact has been no less profound upon the lives they reached.

For much of my adult life some of my more important Spirit Guides have come from a loose collection of American writers and poets who first began finding one another right around the time I was born in 1945. These individuals came to be collectively called the Beat Generation writers. Some of these folk I've been privileged to meet personally; others I only know through their work. I cannot claim any one of them as a personal friend, but I feel a spiritual bond with many of them nonetheless.

The Beats were struggling to breathe freely in what they found to be the socially, culturally, and politically stifling air of post-World War II America. Maybe it was this societal backdrop that caused their quest for *Spiritus* to be so intense. My own coming-of-age era was about one generation removed from that of the Beats, but I find much in their lives and writings that speaks to my own desire for transcendent meaning in the midst of the mundane. I'll be sharing some of their lives and writings in the chapters ahead; but first I am going to share a little of how my spiritual journey has intersected with theirs. I'll start at the time when I was still in the getting-to-know-you phase of my journey with the Beats.

In the summer of 1976 I was cruising around on a houseboat in the delta region of the San Joachin River, east of the San Francisco Bay area. I was spending a month in Berkeley with about a dozen folk in their 20s or 30s. We were getting some training in gestalt therapy from one of Fritz Perls' disciples. He had a large house up in the Berkeley hills where he invited his trainees to live, commune style, for a month while we had our work sessions. In the course of our four weeks together we hit on the idea of renting a houseboat for a weekend as a group get-away.

One particular memory I have of that houseboat trip came back to me with surprising impact as I set out to write this book. I'd completely for-gotten about it. The memory must have remained subconsciously available until I needed it. I recall a beautiful mid-August, mid-California afternoon. I was sitting in an easy chair on the boat's upper deck with my feet propped up on a railing reading Jack Kerouac's *On the Road*. I was still in the early stages of my Kerouac/Beat phase about then, and I'd already read the book a couple of times. I was at it again that day just to add to the pleasure I was experiencing.

One young man in this group from Germany named Josef seemed to derive some special delight in needling me, and he saw my sitting there reading as yet another opportunity. He walked up to me, paused for a few seconds of critical inspection, and after slowly nodding his head a few times as if to indicate he decidedly had my number, said, "You're always *reading* this Kerouac. Why don't you just do it?"

As clearly as I can recall both the setting and Josef's words to me I have absolutely no recollection as to what, if anything, I said back to him. I tend to be a quiet, somewhat introverted, rather taciturn individual. Josef had taken it on, as one of his personal projects, to pull—if not drag—me out of my natural reserve. He saw my reading about the free-spirited, vagabond life that Kerouac celebrates in this novel as the very thing that was keeping me from living such a life.

On the surface Josef may well have had a point. But I wasn't as well versed in Jack Kerouac's life then as I've now come to be. I did not fully grasp at that time how Kerouac also had to deal with a similar dichotomy of the spirit in his own life. He, too, was a largely shy and introverted individual. More often than not he used alcohol to pull himself out of his natural reserve. I've further come to understand that the great spiritual struggle of Kerouac's life—a struggle that encompassed the strict Roman Catholicism in which he was raised and the Buddhism he later came to embrace for a time—was played out in a state of tension. The tension was between his need to be the free-spirited vagabond he celebrated in much of his writings, on the one hand; and the homebody with his books, or sitting in front of his typewriter, while being cared and provided for by his mother, on the other. If I'd been a little more up to speed on the multi-layered, spiritual complexities of Kerouac's life when I was on that houseboat I would have simply said to Josef, "Hey my friend, I'm just living out one of the same paradoxes or contradictions that ol' Jack himself had to deal with."

This is one of the many paradoxes of my life: my need to be a vagabond and my need to be home. It's a paradox I've largely made my peace with after six decades of living. It is also the paradox, or the tension, that has largely fueled and directed my own journey of the soul. Mine is the journey of the restless spiritual pilgrim who still needs to come home now and then. It is the journey of one who needs to move and act, and then stop and reflect and take stock. In a way a houseboat is a good metaphor for such a process.

It is a place to call home even as it moves. And when I find myself caught somewhere between the road and the home, and not quite knowing which turn to take, I see Jack Kerouac—a man I never met in the flesh—giving me a small smile and a knowing nod.

I turned 31 in that American Bicentennial summer of 1976. By then my religious and spiritual odyssey had already taken me across two landscapes, and I was at the boundary marker of a third. My first spiritual home was the one of my upbringing in southern West Virginia, where my parents were devout members of a conservative, evangelical Baptist church. My father was a Deacon; my mother, for many years, was the Church Clerk. Just as Catholicism pervaded Kerouac's early household, the Baptist aura filled up mine. My landscape, in this setting, was one of strict Biblical imperatives and sin-and-salvation revival meetings. As harsh or forbidding as that may sound to the reader, it was actually a safe and loving land. While a visiting evangelist at our week-long spring or fall revival meetings could make things seem pretty scary with his admonitions as to what was in store for the "un-saved," I knew that when he left town I would be back in the care of the kinder and gentler minister of our family church. This minister showed a special interest in me. I wanted to be like him when I grew up. He baptized me, in the total immersion method that Baptists use, when I was ten years old; and a few years later I confided to him that I, too, wanted to follow the path to ministry. He and my parents were very proud of me.

Around the middle of my college years my spiritual landscape changed. I took a rather sharp turn to the left towards a more liberal, academic, social-activist brand of American Protestantism. If I were to do an association exercise portraying my spiritual journey during my college days the list would include: Campus chaplains, Vatican II, folk-music services, the ecumenical movement, interfaith retreats, the early civil rights and peace movements, the campus coffee house, the early songs of Bob Dylan as sung by Peter, Paul, and Mary, and the alleged Death of God. Out of this milieu I chose to enter a very liberal Protestant theological school in upstate New York in the late 1960s. I was ordained as an American Baptist minister in 1971, and went on to become a campus chaplain myself.

Towards the latter part of my seminary years I began reading Kerouac. I discovered him right about the time he died in 1969 when I read *The Dharma*

Bums. As an English major, when I'd find a writer whose work appealed to me I'd read as much as I could of him or her. So it was with Kerouac. I took on the rest of his *oeuvre* in the ensuing years.

For those who read the comic strip *Doonesbury,* I call the few years I spent in the campus ministry my Rev. Scot Sloan Days. As it turned out those years were pretty short lived. By the mid-70s I'd become restless again in the landscape of liberal Christianity and found myself being drawn to yet another piece of territory. The humanistic psychology movement was coming into its heyday about this time, and it struck a resonant chord in me. Since the San Francisco Bay area, along with the Esalen Institute, was the unofficial headquarters of this movement, I headed to the West Coast for a couple of summers. That's how I found myself on a houseboat reading Kerouac.

By the summer of 1976 I had come to a pivotal and in-between place in my life. I was somewhere between the terrain of liberal Christianity and agnostic humanism. On a more personal note I was, as things turned out, between marriages. Being in this in-between place, in fact, caused me to take a hiatus from the ministry about a year later. The concept of God as an intentional Supreme Being no longer worked for me. Agnostic Humanist seemed to describe me best.

But if traditional theism was no longer viable for me, I found that atheism left a spiritual void. In ways that I did not fully recognize or appreciate at the time, it was my explorations into the life and writings of Jack Kerouac that helped to fill this void. In time these explorations would introduce me to the wider cultural and literary phenomenon which, by the mid-70s, was already being referred to in the past tense, i.e. the Beat Generation. But it's funny how things turn out. Culturally speaking the Beats are more present tense now than they were during the 1970s; and, on a more personal level, they have continued to guide my spiritual path as it keeps taking its twists and turns.

Time passes. Some twenty-five years after Josef put his question to me on the houseboat I found myself posing it in a slightly different way in a sermon I offered on the Beat Generation to the Unitarian Universalist congregation I now serve in Nashua, New Hampshire. I put it this way: "What is a middle-aged, middle-class, unassuming nice guy like me doing being so attracted to a bunch of crazy people who were having their heyday during my pre-teen years?" It was not the first time I'd tossed out a largely rhetorical question in a sermon for which I had no quick or easy reply. Indeed it's a question I'm still answering for myself ever since I happened upon that copy of *The Dharma Bums* back in '69. While reading that book something took hold of me and has never let me go. After Kerouac, I started in on poets and writers like Allen Ginsberg, Lawrence Ferlinghetti, Gary Snyder, William S. Burroughs, Diane di Prima, and numerous others who have been grouped under the umbrella term of The Beat Generation. I found these writers, each with his or her own unique style, were speaking to the same kind of spiritual restlessness I was experiencing.

As noted I came of age during the tumult of the 1960s, with all of its exuberance and melancholy, hope and despair, as well as its promises and its ashes. Even as I prepared for the ministry in the liberal Protestant tradition I seriously wondered where and how I was going to find a place in a world that was turning upside down. I consider it fortuitous that I discovered at that same time a constellation of writers and poets who actually celebrated and delighted in being misfits! Maybe "fitting in" wasn't, or didn't have to be, the be-all and end-all of existence. I was captivated by the daring and off-beat energy, as well as the intimacy, of the literary creations of these folk. After reading *On the Road* I felt like I'd spent an evening in a bar listening to Jack Kerouac spin his tale for me over a few beers, and I wanted to go find him so we could continue the conversation. Although, tragically enough, Kerouac was dead by then we still have our conversations.

What I was picking up from Kerouac and the other Beats was something that ran far deeper than the good buzz one gets from good writing. In ways I couldn't precisely put my finger on, I found spiritual searches and affirmations, as well as soulful yearnings, contained within these Beat writings that touched and taught me in ways that most of my seminary texts and courses had not. While the Beats wrote largely out of a sense of alienation and estrangement from much of the American cultural ethos of the post-World War II 1950s, they eschewed the near nihilism of the post-World War I Lost Generation. They believed that there was a Holy or Sacred dimension to Life Itself to be uncovered. This dimension could be found somewhere beneath the cultural conformity and banality they sensed was increasingly coming to define the soul and character of America as they were coming of age.

Some two decades after the Beat constellation first began forming I found myself in a similar existential place, somewhere between personal estrangement and a reaching for the Holy. When I got to that aforementioned boundary marker between the lands of liberal Christianity and agnostic humanism, it was the Beats—especially Jack Kerouac, Allen Ginsberg, and Gary Snyder—who served as reminders to me that one can doubt or deny the existence of a Supreme Being and still need, and pursue, a spiritual connection with all of Being.

When Allen Ginsberg first read his epic work *Howl* to a gathering of fledging poets and writers in San Francisco in October of 1955, I was a ten year old kid who'd barely been outside the borders of West Virginia. Nearly a decade and a half later, however, I felt a little too old to be a Hippie as that era reached its full flower (pun intended). Besides, by the time I reached my mid-twenties I'd gained enough self-knowledge to know that I wasn't altogether cut out for the bohemian lifestyle which the Beats, to greater or lesser degrees, epitomized. I knew I wanted, and chose to pursue, the security props that many of us look for at that time in our lives: a career, a family, a reasonably well assured source of income, and at least the broad outline of a reliable road-map for the course of our lives. I value these things.

But there remained in me a Beat consciousness, as I like to call it, that I also value. I could tamp that consciousness down, but never fully extinguish it. Within my personal realm of awareness and yearnings, there was at least one little light that wanted nothing more than the opportunity to live my life "on the road" without the encumbrances of all those security props. In many respects my spiritual journey is one that has grown out of the tension between these two needs and desires, even as did Jack Kerouac's.

Metaphorically, and literally, speaking it is that tension between the home and the road. It's the tension found in the very title of the first novel of Kerouac's first published novel, *The Town and the City*, which came out in 1950. *The Town and the City* is a straight prose novel in which Kerouac aspires to attain the literary voice of Thomas Wolfe, before finding a literary voice of his own. In the book he calls the town Galloway, and patterns it after his own hometown of Lowell, Massachusetts. The city is New York.

The central character in the book is Peter Martin, who also represents Kerouac's persona. Peter is a member of the rather large Martin family, an expanded version of Jack's comparatively small Kerouac family of origin. Much of the book centers on the often stormy, but still loving, relationship between Peter and his father, George Martin; just as Jack and his father, Leo Kerouac, had their own stormy-yet-loving relationship. Peter loves Galloway/Lowell but finds he cannot live there, just as he loves his father but still has to leave the Martin household. He comes to live in New York City where he finds a life for himself within a close circle of friends, even as Kerouac did at that same time.

But Peter is restless, wherever he happens to be. He needs both the town and the city, but he cannot remain in either one. At the conclusion of the novel George Martin dies, and is brought back to the Martin family's burial plot in the town of Lacoshua (Nashua), New Hampshire. With his father gone, and now free from his father's expectations, Peter sets out on his own, still looking, searching, and needing:

> Peter was alone in the rainy night. He was on the road again, travel-ing the continent westward, going off to further and further years, alone by the waters of life...looking down along the shore in remembrance of the dearness of his father and all of life...When the railroad trains moaned, and river-winds blew, bringing echoes through the vale, it was as if a wild hum of voices, the dear voices of everybody he had known, were crying: "Peter, Peter! Where are you going Peter?"

Jack Kerouac was 25 years old when he wrote these words. By the end of the novel Peter Martin is roughly the same age. Through him, Kerouac speaks of his ongoing spiritual struggle, his need for a sense of place, and yet his competing need to hear and respond to the call of the unknown. But Peter Martin is also any person of any age who finds him or herself alone in that breach between the equally demanding, and equally valid, need for roots and for wings. Even in the sixth decade of my life, I have not ceased being Peter Martin. I still move between the town and the city: the security and predictability of the town, the adventure and open-endedness of the city, and the call of mystery and the unknown (i.e. the road). These are the components of any journey of the spirit. This is why a novel like *The Town and the City* continues to speak to my own human experience at whatever point in the human life-cycle I may be.

Over the years, then, Kerouac and many of the other Beat writers informed my own journey of the soul in two essential ways. First they have allowed me to understand, and even appreciate, the bargain I have made with Life. Second, they have shown me the way of the Holy and the Sacred in the midst of the mundane.

For the curious human mind it is the ordinariness of Life, in fact, that really presents the greatest challenge in living. Yes, many people remake their lives and find relief in the ordinary after horrible tragedies and losses. And many of them rise to that rebuilding challenge in ways that still astound me. But the challenge of finding meaning in the day-to-dayness of living can also be daunting. We human beings are both blessed and cursed with the ability to dream dreams and to imagine lives other than the lives we live. To invoke a rather un-Beat reference here, in 1972 the Statler Brothers came out with a song called *The Class of '57 Had Its Dreams*. The chorus goes like this:

> And the Class of Fifty Seven had its dreams.
> But we all thought we'd change the world
> With our great works and deeds;
> Or maybe we just thought the world
> Would change to fit our needs.
> The Class of Fifty Seven had its dreams.

Here's one of the verses:

> Helen is a hostess,
> Frank works at the mill,
> Janet teaches grade school
> And prob'ly always will.
> Bob works for the city
> And Jack's in lab research
> And Betty plays the organ
> At the Presbyterian Church

The song ends with these lines:

> But livin' life from day to day
> Is never like it seems.
> Things get complicated

THE BEAT FACE OF GOD

When you get past eighteen,
But the Class of Fifty Seven had its dreams.

In a collection of his essays titled *Palm Sunday* the novelist Kurt Vonnegut suggests that this Statler Brothers song be made our National Anthem. It's a quintessential Vonnegut crack—sardonic and serious at the same time. Vonnegut also uses this song to get in a playful dig at Allen Ginsberg, when he, Vonnegut, asserts that *The Class of '57* speaks far more accurately to the experience of the World War II, and immediate post-World War II, generation than does Ginsberg's *Howl*. Perhaps Vonnegut is right. The Statler Brothers are addressing a more widely felt sentiment with this song than Ginsberg does with *Howl*. But both pieces of writing speak to that craving, that paradox of security versus exploration, and of dreams versus the ordinary.

The Class of '57 is about the bargains we make, or the deals we have to cut with life. Things do indeed get complicated when one gets past 18—or 25 for those who use college and graduate school to extend the formation of their dreams, ideals, yearnings, and fantasies. At some point the reality sets in that the world isn't going to "change to fit our needs," and that most of the adapting is going to have to be ours instead. Okay, so the bargain goes, I'll play by the rules: pursue a career; raise a family; buy and maintain a house; be a responsible and contributing member of the community. In return one gets the security and the acceptance, and yes, the satisfaction and the personal fulfillment that these things can indeed bring.

But somewhere in the recesses of our soul we know that even when the deal pays off like it is supposed to, we're still a little short. We may not be able to fully comprehend, or adequately give voice to, exactly what that shortness is about; we just know it's there. For many of us there is still a part of us that continues to reach beyond the deal, even if we do not fully know what we might end up holding

The Beats were the ones who would not, or could not, cut the deal or make the bargain. If *The Class of '57* is an acknowledgement of the bargain, then *Howl* is the Great Refusal of the bargain. *On the Road*, with its heady mix of wild abandonment along with its intimations of tragedy, is both a "no" to the bargain and a "yes" to running the risks of refusal. Kerouac's novel was published, by the way, in 1957.

Some of the Beats paid dearly and tragically for their refusal, while others lived to prevail over it. Some of them actually were able to change their immediate worlds to fit their needs. Whatever their various fates have proven to be they were trying to get out the same message that Jesus (whom I regard as a proto-Beat) conveyed to his followers: "Life is more than food and the body more than clothing." Hear Allen Ginsberg again: "I write poetry because the English word Inspiration comes from Latin *Spiritus*, breath. I want to breathe freely." So do most of us. For all the deals we may cut with life, we still need to inhale the Breath of Life. The Beats provided a life-line for those whose spirits needed to breathe during the 1950s. The line remains open.

For many of the Beats, their refusal to limit their journeys and their possibilities was a refusal made for the sake of a greater affirmation. This is an affirmation of Holiness. Earlier in this chapter I alluded to three landscapes of my spiritual journey. Now I am finding my way into a fourth Landscape of the Spirit. While I have not returned to traditional Theism I am again learning, however gingerly, to speak of God. God, as I now use the name, is the Presence of the Holy, the Divine, or the Sacred within our world and universe in which we live and move and have our being. We can know and access this Presence if we remain open to its intimations. The ten dollar word for this stance is *panentheism*. I'm pretty sure that none of the Beats ever used such a term, but it does describe the religious or spiritual dimension contained in much of their writing. Panentheism is the theological perspective from which I write this book.

The Beats spoke in terms of their personal religious roots and still grew beyond them. Kerouac, to be sure, remained enough of a Catholic throughout his life that he never completely let go of his belief in a Supreme Being Deity. But his writing, especially what he produced during the Buddhist phase of his life, celebrates a Sacredness embedded in the world instead of a judgmental, patriarchal God who rules over the world. Much of Ginsberg's work encompasses the roles of prophet and priest. Raised in the Jewish faith, he does at times come on like an Old Testament prophet railing against the evils of his day. But Ginsberg, too, developed an attachment to Buddhism that caused him to take the meditative and contemplative life seriously. Gary Snyder was raised in the rural Pacific Northwest where he cultivated a neo-pagan, earth based spirituality, and then became a serious student and practitioner of Zen Buddhism. There is a certain whimsical and light-hearted quality to much of Snyder's writings, even as he puts his readers in touch with the Spirit. In his poem *Marin-An* he recounts the act of eating oysters in both a playful and profound way that becomes a description of a Eucharistic partaking of the Holy.

I first discovered the Beats during my sojourn in the land of Liberal Christianity. They kept growing on me during my years in the land of Agnostic Humanism. Now they are helping usher me into the land of Panentheism. They have been my Spirit Guides. Jack Kerouac, Allen Ginsberg, and Gary Snyder have been among the stronger influences on my spiritual journey. But a number of others continue to influence me as well. I offer the guidance they've given me in the hope that others may find take some direction from them as well.

In closing, I return once more to the paradox, or the yin/yang, with which I've lived for most of my life. A big part of me wants the furniture to be in the same place every time I walk into my house. Another part of me could do without the house altogether. The Beats have been, and remain, the siren-song voices for the part of me that will not put all of my eggs in the basket of predictability and stability.

In a well-known episode in Homer's *Odyssey,* the hero Odysseus orders his fellow sailors to strap him to the mast of his ship so he can hear the songs of the Sirens but not succumb to their enticements, and thereby abandon his journey home to his family and his settled life. It would less than honest for me to say that I've been strapped to a mast for the last 30 plus years of my life. My family, my career in the ministry, and the house I've helped to maintain over the years have all brought me joy and fulfillment, along with the inevitable frustrations, pains, and let-downs.

But I know why Odysseus did what he did. He needed to hear other voices even though he knew he could not fully follow their call. He needed to hear the beat of another drum even if he could not allow himself to com-pletely step to it. I, too, need to hear another beat. And in my own way, I do step to it.

CHAPTER THREE

Jack Kerouac and the Face of God

I got the request through the contact link of the website for the Lowell Celebrates Kerouac Organization. A gentleman from San Francisco, Mike, logged in saying he had a business trip coming up in Boston the following week, and he wanted to come up to Lowell to see what he could find of Jack Kerouac. "Is there someone in your organization who can take me to his gravesite, and maybe show me some of the places he writes about in his Lowell based novels?" he asked. It so happened that I was free on the Saturday that Mike wanted to come to Lowell, so I agreed to meet him and show him around.

We met at the Visitors Center at the Lowell Historic National Park. Mike had a couple of his Boston based friends with him who were more or less along for the ride. The four of us, three guys and a young woman, struck up an easy going kind of camaraderie as we drove around town.

We visited the Kerouac Commemorative in downtown Lowell, Kerouac's birthplace on Lupine Road in Lowell's Centerville section, and the house on Beaulieu Street where the Kerouac family lived when Jack was four years old. After a few stops at some of the Kerouac places in some of Lowell's other neighborhoods, we came to the St. Jean Baptiste Church where Kerouac's Funeral Mass was held on October 23, 1969, two days after the author's death in St. Petersburg, Florida.

Mike was taking pictures the whole time. But keeping his face behind his camera allowed him to hide a kind of pensive mood, combined with a tinge of sadness. His friends probably missed it, but I had no trouble recognizing the look. It was the same one I had on my face when I'd made my first Kerouac pilgrimage to Lowell some 20 years earlier. Mike might have thought he was coming to Lowell as a tourist—maybe that was even what he'd told his friends when they'd set out from Boston that morning—but now he was a pilgrim who was finally being able to make his journey of faith to a sacred spot.

Our last stop was the Edson Cemetery where Jack Kerouac is buried. The marker at the gravesite lies flush to the ground. You can't find it by looking around for Kerouac's name on an upraised stone. The name on the marker is "John L. Kerouac." The three word epitaph reads, "He honored life." He is buried next to his wife, Stella Sampas Kerouac, who passed away in 1990 and whose name is also on the marker. I led my three newly-met companions to the spot. As soon as he saw the marker Mike dropped to his knees—the same reflexive motion a Catholic makes in the church aisle before moving into a pew and then kneeling again. Mike remained motionless for nearly half a minute, apparently not even aware that his knees were sinking into the wet ground of a cold New England February day.

The other three of us, also in a collective reflexive motion, took a few steps backward. We instinctively knew that to stand too close to Mike at this moment would be an invasion of the sacred space he'd created. Whatever business demands had brought him from San Francisco to Boston, the real reason and meaning of his trip to the East Coast was now being fulfilled. In time he stood up and smiled at us and resumed the conversation we'd been having while walking from my car to the grave. Mike seemed a little surprised, and perhaps even a tad embarrassed, at the effect the sight of Kerouac's grave had on him. I don't believe he was quite prepared for how he would react. Now he needed to break the spell, both for himself as well as for the rest of us.

We talked a bit longer. I told him and his friends about some of the more interesting notes, letters, and poems—as well as the various artifacts (mostly wine and whiskey bottles)—that I've found placed on this grave over the years that I've visited. I drove them back to where they'd parked their car. After the thank-yous and the good-byes we all went on our ways.

The scene I witnessed, and was a part of, on that sunny and cold winter morning is one I know has been replayed many times over with visitors from all over the world. More often than not it's a scene that goes unnoticed. When I made my first such pilgrimage to Lowell in 1974, alone and on a warm New England summer day, my mood was much like that of Mike's. I, too, took pictures while feeling I was on a holy journey. When I got to the grave site I, too, reflexively knelt down just as Mike had done, before I even knew what I was doing. Perhaps the most familiar picture of Kerouac's grave is the one that shows Allen Ginsberg and a very young Bob Dylan sitting in a meditative mode—with Dylan strumming a guitar—on the very same spot where Mike and I and hundreds, if not thousands of others, have paid their respects and offered their prayers over the years since Jack was laid to rest there at the age of 47.

What is the draw here? From Bob Dylan to the young junior executive that Mike appeared to be, to aspiring writers and lovers of literature, to those who are "on the road" themselves and feel this is a stop they have to make, they all come to Kerouac's grave. On one of my visits to the Edson Cemetery I found, under a rock next to the marker, a long, pencil-scrawled letter to Jack from a wandering soul who was trying to get from somewhere in Maine to the West Coast. He had written this long explanation to Kerouac about why he was making the trip.

Since I'm the one raising the question, I should ask it of myself: Why do I keep going back there? Why do I make it a point to be at the Kerouac gravesite each year on March 12, his birthday, and October 21, the date of his death? Perhaps the draw to this site is the same thing that brings together the people I see in front of me on a Sunday morning when I stand up to lead a worship service. I see men and women—of a wide age range—who are looking for what the theologian Paul Tillich called the "depth dimension" to life. They are concerned with matters of spirituality, with what it means—and feels like—to be connected to a Reality, a Power, Presence, or a Force that is greater than themselves even if they cannot fully conceive or grasp what this mysterious It is. They may even call this Elusive It, God; although the name is not that important. They come because they feel there has to be something, some meaning, beyond the mundaneness that characterizes much of the life around us. This search, in the end, is what has always drawn persons to religion and to the search for spirituality. But what does any of this have to do with a grave marker in a city cemetery in Lowell, Massachusetts, for a writer who died in alcoholic obscurity in a St. Petersburg, Florida hospital in the waning months of the 1960s?

Well, it's not really about the cemetery or the marker, however powerful an effect the locale may have. It's about one man's search for meaning and a place for himself. It's about his search for peace of mind as well as for the excitement of living. Those who come to Kerouac's grave search for these same things. Kerouac, along with many of his literary companions and soul-mates, refused to accept the pre-packaged blueprints for life and meaning that were being foisted upon them, and decided that they would discover for themselves what is Ultimate about life. People visit Kerouac's grave, read his works, and identify with his life because they connect with his struggle, and with the struggle of his fellow Beats. They also want to connect with the joy that emerged in the midst of his deep awareness of sadness and tragedy. To read *On the Road* with any kind of care and deliberation is to hear the book's undertone of sad yearning that underlies any quest for meaning. The wild exuberance, and the sometimes careening craziness, that are often touted as what the book is "really all about, man," are actually the book's occasional counter-points to the basic loneliness of any journey of the soul. As Kerouac himself said on the Steve Allen Show in the crazed aftermath of *On the Road's* publication, "I wrote the book because we're all going to die." Which is to say, I'm trying to squeeze some life out of life while I still have life to live. This is what those who go to Kerouac's grave are also doing.

Kerouac, as he was about to be consumed by the demons of celebrity-hood when *On the Road* became a best-seller, found himself on a New York City radio talk-show called *Nightbeat*. The host was trying to entice what-ever juicy sound-bites he could out of the newly famous writer. Jack was asked what it was he and this Beat Generation really wanted. Kerouac said, "I am waiting for God to show me his face." He would later expand upon this remark in an essay called *Lion, No Lamb*:

> After publishing my book about the beat generation I was asked to explain beatness on TV, on radio, by people everywhere…What are you searching for? they asked me. I answered that I was waiting for God to show his face. I (said) that even mad happy hepcats…were creatures of God laid out here in this infinite universe without knowing what for.

And besides, I've never heard more talk about God among the kids of my generation; and not the intellectual kids alone, all of them. In the faces of my questioners was the hopeless question: Why?..

I believe that Kerouac's writings, and those of other Beats, were an attempt to answer the "what for?" of life. This, I claim, is what Kerouac meant when he said he wanted God to show his face. But rather than spin out philosophical or theological or intellectual sounding discourses Kerouac pointed his readers to the holy and the sacred that he believed were contained in the natural world of people and nature and events in which we all live. This, indeed, is the role and task of the artist: to point to the sacred and the holy that dwell within the life of the culture in which she or he lives. By sacred and holy I do not mean some other realm of existence that is sealed off from the here and now and for which you need permission to enter. The role of the artist, the poet, the writer is to allow us to see that sacred dimension to life that has always been right in front of us. It is to allow us, in T.S. Eliot's words, "to arrive at where we started and see it clearly for the first time." I call sacred or holy that which lifts us out of ourselves—if only for a moment—and lets us see the preciousness of life and our connection to the Larger Life that surrounds and enfolds us.

"I want God to show me his face." Kerouac's own religion, as it comes through to his readers, was a mixture of his early Catholicism, his near immersion in Buddhism for a time, plus some philosophical and spiritual meanderings of his own. Without knowing for sure, I'll take my guess at what he meant with those words. Maybe he was trying to say: I want to know what really matters. I want to know what it is that ultimately pulls together this mad, crazy and tangled life of mine. I want to know how and where I find the sacred beneath and beyond the ordinary, and beyond the personal life that is confounding me. In other words, I want God to show his face.

Whether they used Kerouac's language or not, I think this is what the Beats themselves were looking for—the face of God. By "God" I do not mean they were searching for a Deity or a Supreme Being with a Divine Will and a Divine Plan for their lives. Instead I mean they sought an immediacy with life.

The Beat Credo was actually stated over a century prior to their era by

Henry David Thoreau when he said, " I want to learn what life has to teach, and not, when I come to die, discover that I have not lived...I want to live deep and suck out all the marrow of life." Allen Ginsberg updated this credo for those of his own generation when he termed his contemporaries, in his poem *Howl*, "angelheaded hipsters burning for the ancient heavenly connection to the starry dynamo."

The theological term for this kind of approach to God and spirituality was cited in the previous chapter, *panentheism*. The word has an academic and unwieldy sound to it, and I'm sure the Beats never heard or used it. But I believe they were exponents of it. Panentheism refers to the Presence of God within the material or the ordinary. Don't confuse it with pantheism which holds that all of existence is synonymous with God, or that the entire material world is a manifestation of God. Panentheism affirms, as indicated, that there is something of the Sacred or the Holy embedded within the ordinary. It is analogous to Ralph Waldo Emerson's well known dictum that we each have within us a "spark of the Divine." Emerson was not saying that we're all Gods, but rather that we have something of the Godly within us and that we can, at times, connect with our "Godly Something." Panentheism does not hold that all is God, but rather that something of God is contained in All That Is.

Another of my ministerial colleagues, the Rev. William F. Schulz, has articulated this stance quite well with these words:

> The Sacred or the Divine, the Precious and the Profound are made evident not in the miraculous or the supernatural, but in the simple and the everyday. The gracious is available to every one of us, disguised in the simple and the mundane.

Or as Dean Moriarty (Neal Cassady) says to Sal Paradise (Jack Kerouac) in *On the Road*, "Troubles, you see, is the generalization-word for what God exists in."

Perhaps it is the desire to find the gracious, disguised in the simple, or the God who exists in our troubles, that draws so many people to the grave of Jack Kerouac. His is one simple marker in the middle of acres and acres of thousands of other such markers. But it has also become a piece of the larger spiritual mosaic of the culture of the late twentieth and now early twenty-first centuries.

Seeking the face of God—so to speak—without, I hope, trivializing or demeaning the matter, has become something of a growth industry in our time. Evangelical Christianity is enjoying a boomlet of its own but it speaks to only one component of the larger spiritual mosaic of our culture. Weekend spiritual growth workshops of one type or another have become a basic staple of our society. The Vietnamese Zen Buddhist monk, Thich Nhat Hahn, set up an American retreat center near Woodstock, Vermont. The 12 Step Recovery process, originally created for those seeking to rescue their lives from the grip of alcoholism, becomes a spiritual path in and of itself for millions. And the writings of a man, who lost his own battle with alcoholism and who had been largely dismissed as a literary has-been in the early 1970s, are discovered and read by a generation of people who had not been born at the time of his death. These people include my young companion-for-a-day, Mike, who by all indications has made it in the culture of contemporary America. He crossed the continent to kneel at the grave of Jack Kerouac.

We didn't discuss religion during our brief visit, but perhaps Mike, too, in the midst of his life, wants to see the face of God.

"In the faces of my questioners was the hopeless question: But why?" wrote Jack Kerouac in the wild aftermath of the publication of *On the Road*, when, as he put it, "everything exploded." But the question is never to be fully answered, just as the face of God is never to be fully revealed. The important thing, however, is that Jack Kerouac made the effort. And the even more important thing, as I'm sure he'd tell us himself if he could, is that we make the effort for ourselves as well.

I turn to Kerouac when I need some encouragement in making the effort myself. Whether it's a visit to his grave—which is about a half-hour's drive from my home—or simply reflecting upon his joyful and tragic, ebullient and troubled, divine and demonic life, I need to say "thank you" to him now and again. I thank him for pointing out a precious kind of beauty in the tired and forlorn face of a diner waitress. I thank him for seeing a strange kind of saintliness in the often wild and crazy ways of his companion of the road, Neal Cassady. I thank him for allowing me to see a land I can still love, even with what all its politicians have done to it, through the window of a Greyhound bus. I thank him for noticing the spurting froth on the rocks of the Merrimack River as it flowed through his home town of Lowell, even as it now flows alongside of mine. I thank him for having the courage to recount his own dark nights of the soul on Washington State's Desolation Peak and at California's Big Sur. For in each of these revelations Kerouac offers at least a fleeting glimpse of that elusive face of God, and a passing intimation of the Divine that resides in the ordinary and even, at times, in the destructive.

Jack Kerouac died a lonely death, and one that gave the appearance of a defeated man. But his life and literary legacy have proven to be far more lasting in the years following his death than in those preceeding it. While he died in isolation, his spirit now touches the lives of countless individuals—many of whom make the trip to Lowell to pay their respects and offer their thanks to Jack Kerouac.

My most lasting memory of a trip to his grave came on one of my March 12 birthday treks following an especially severe New England winter. The snow was so deep and wet that I did not want to make the walk from the roadway that passes near his grave to the marker itself. I stood in the roadway and offered a silent prayer in the direction of Kerouac's grave. About five or six young people, probably in their teens and twenties, approached. None of them were wearing boots. Without breaking stride they walked through the knee-deep snow and formed a circle around the marker. From their pockets each of them took out a poem s/he'd written, and read it as they stood in their circle. Then they tromped back through the snow and continued on their way.

God, Jack, if you only could have seen it.

Maybe you did.

CHAPTER FOUR

Divine Madness, Demonic Madness, and the Holy

I saw the best minds of my generation destroyed by madness.
Allen Ginsberg. *Howl.*

The only people for me are the mad ones.
Jack Kerouac. *On the Road.*

*S*cientific American is not a publication that often gets onto my peri-
odical reading list. It is a top quality journal, but most of its pieces are
well beyond my range of understanding and expertise. The February,
1995 issue, however, did catch my attention due to a fascinating article that
explored the connection between artistic, poetic, and literary creativity and
certain forms of mental illness or madness. [*Manic Depressive Illness and
Creativity* by Kay Redfield Jamison.]

The article opened with a quote from Edgar Allen Poe: "Men have called
me mad. But the question is not yet settled whether madness is or is not the
loftiest intelligence..." Granted, it was hardly a novel topic. The fine line that
often runs between the creative drive and the drive towards self-destruction in certain individuals is one that has been long recognized and scruti-
nized. The text of the piece proved to be basic *Scientific American* fare: lots
of charts, graphs, and survey results demonstrating how there are higher
rates of suicide, depression, and manic depression among writers, artists,
and poets than in the general population.

The pictures on the first couple of pages of the article, however, were more captivating than the text. These pages contained a large photographic collage of well known writers and artists who were either diagnosed as manic-depressives or showed signs of it. Others pictured had had their battles with alcoholism or addictive drugs. Among those shown were Vincent Van Gogh, Sylvia Plath, Anne Sexton, Walt Whitman, Edgar Allen Poe, Tennessee Williams, Ernest Hemingway, and Mark Twain.

Neither Allen Ginsberg nor Jack Kerouac were among those pictured. Yet they each had their encounters with madness, and their lives and their work were shaped by those encounters. At age 23 Allen spent several months in New York's Columbia Presbyterian Psychiatric Institute as an alternative to going to jail. Thanks to his naive good will towards Hubert Huncke, introduced in Chapter One, Allen found himself the inadvertent party to a series of robberies since Huncke was stashing the goods in Allen's apartment. Ginsberg was struggling with his sexual orientation at the time, believing that he was homosexual but not quite able to accept it. At a time when most young men of his age were finding their societal niche, Ginsberg was having serious doubts as to whether there was any rightful place where he could fit in and feel normal.

About a year prior to his committal Ginsberg had had a vision wherein he'd heard the voice of the eighteenth-century British poet William Blake reading his (Blake's) poetry to Ginsberg. This experience caused the young Mr. Ginsberg to run through the streets of New York informing anyone whom he happened to encounter that he'd seen God. It was the most profound spiritual experience of Ginsberg's life to that point and he was still struggling to determine what it might portend for him. The prescription he got from the Psychiatric Institute doctors, however, was that he was a brilliant, near genius-level, individual who needed to "cure" himself of his homosexuality and divest himself of his subterranean circle of aspiring poets and writers who were leading him astray from the productive life he could be living.

Six years prior Kerouac had also found himself, for a short time, confined to a psychiatric ward. At the onset of America's entry into World War II Kerouac enlisted in the Navy, in February of 1943, following a run on the *USS Dorchester* for the United States Merchant Marine. He found he was utterly unable to adjust to the regimentation of military life. During a boot camp drill at the U. S. Naval Base in Newport, Rhode Island, Kerouac set his rifle down on the field and walked off to the base library to read.

He was not making any kind of political statement or lodging any kind of protest; he simply could not follow the drill regimen. In a way Jack was replicating on this naval base what he'd often done a few years earlier during his senior year at Lowell High School. Instead of showing up for his prescribed classes, he would skip school and spend the day the Lowell's Pollard Library reading whatever works were of interest to him.

But the United States Navy isn't Lowell High School. Kerouac was immediately sent to the psychiatric ward of the base hospital, and some weeks later was transferred to a Navy psychiatric hospital in Bethesda, Maryland. Five months after his initial infraction Kerouac was diagnosed by the Navy doctors as having "schizoid tendencies" and was released from the United States Navy on psychiatric grounds, albeit with an honorable discharge with a notation of "indifferent character."

While the circumstances surrounding the respective hospitalizations of Ginsberg and Kerouac were markedly different, the assumption and diagnosis made in both of their cases was that because they could not adequately adapt to the values and ethos of the culture within which they each found themselves, they were therefore mentally ill. As will be shown in a later chapter, mental illness has been a common diagnosis of women who do not fit the cultural expectations of their day. This was especially true of some of the women who chose to follow their own beat in America during the 1950s.

Mental illness is, let there be no doubt, a crippling and often devastating malady. It has shattered lives and families. One significant indicator of any society's level of compassion is found in how it treats and deals with its mentally ill citizens. That said, however, the term "mentally ill" can also be used as a handy pigeon-hole category or label by a society that doesn't quite know what to do with some of its more creative misfits. Just label them mentally ill and make conformity the cure. So, an inability to fully adapt to the cultural ethos of a given society at any given point in its history should not be automatically equated with mental illness.

What Ginsberg and Kerouac did with the diagnoses given them is telling. Ginsberg concluded, six years after his psychiatric incarceration when he set out to write his signature work, *Howl*, that the real madness was found in a society that was destroying "the best minds of my generation." His poem goes on for stanza after stanza as something of a raw scream at what Ginsberg saw as the demonic madness of his day. Ginsberg's scream was directed at some of the more destructive forces and powers of the America of the mid-1950s with its Cold War fears, its race for nuclear superiority, and its fanatical, fear-laden anti-communism. The poem also heralds those who lived on the fringes of society at that time and who, like him, would have been classified as madmen. Ginsberg dedicated the poem to a man he met in the Psychiatric Institute, Carl Solomon, who became his life-long friend. *Howl* is not a piece of poetry for the squeamish or faint-hearted.

The first section of *Howl* draws upon both Ginsberg's personal experiences and those of his friends and compatriots as he moves from literal to poetic to metaphorical levels, sometimes in the same line, as he describes the fates of some of these best minds:

Who poverty and tatters and hollow-eyed and high sat up smoking in the supernatural darkness of cold-water flats floating across the tops of cities contemplating jazz,

Who bared their brains to Heaven under the El and saw Mohammedan angles staggering on tenement roofs illuminated,

Who cowered in unshaven rooms in underwear, burning their money in wastebaskets and listening to the Terror through the wall...

In the second section of the poem Ginsberg calls down his wrath upon Moloch in a manner that resembles some of the Old Testament prophets calling down the wrath of Yahweh upon those who have strayed from the ways of the Lord. With reference to all of those about whom he'd written in the first section, Ginsberg opens Section Two of *Howl* by asking:

What sphinx of cement and aluminum bashed open their skulls and ate up their brains and imagination?

[The culprit is Moloch], whose mind is pure machinery! ...whose eyes are a thousand blind windows! ...whose factories dream and croak in the fog ...whose smokestacks and antennae crown the cities!

Moloch is a Canaanite Deity referred to in the Old Testament books of II Kings and Jeremiah. He was one who had to be appeased or propitiated by the sacrificial burning of children. In Ginsberg's vision/nightmare, Moloch is his metaphor for the destructive dimension of an emerging corporate/industrial society that required the lives and souls of its members in order to function and grow.

In Section Three of *Howl* Ginsberg expresses his solidarity with one-time fellow inmate at the Psychiatric Institute, Carl Solomon—"Carl Solomon! I am with you in Rockland where you are madder than I am"—as a way of making common cause with those who stand accused of madness for simply trying to maintain their sanity in the land of Moloch.

While the original poem ended with the Carl Solomon Section, Ginsberg later added a *Footnote to Howl* wherein he affirms the essential holiness of life; a holiness that is contained within the horror: "Holy the solitudes of skyscrapers and pavements! Holy the cafeterias filled with the millions! Holy the mysterious river of tears under the streets!"

The poem, taken in its entirety, is a journey through madness and terror, enroute to the holy. There is sanctity of life that one can get to, provided one is willing, and has the courage, to walk through and face down all that would deny that sanctity. This is the message Ginsberg sought to convey with this work.

While Kerouac greatly admired Ginsberg's *Howl*, he took a different tack. For him the emphasis was upon madness as something to be celebrated. In one sense, *On the Road* picks up where *Howl* leaves off. That is to say, Kerouac begins his work with an affirmation of the holy madness at which Ginsberg arrives at the end of *Howl*. After several cross-country treks, sometimes by himself and sometimes with his companion of the road, Neal Cassady, Kerouac set out to write his first complete draft of *On the Road* in April of 1951. He did it in a three week marathon at the typewriter using a continuous roll of paper so he would not lose his concentration by having to change sheets. For those three weeks, so the story goes, he subsisted largely on black coffee and Benzedrine and hardly any sleep, which was an exercise in madness all by itself.

The best known and most often quoted lines Kerouac produced in that outburst of writing, while in a semi-mad state of his own, are found in the early pages of the work:

The only people for me are the mad ones, the ones who are mad to live, mad to talk, mad to be saved, desirous of everything at the same time, the ones who never yawn or say a commonplace thing, but burn, burn, burn like fabulous roman candles exploding like spiders across the skies and in the middle you see the blue centerlight pop and everybody goes "awwww!..."

As a counterpoint to the demonic madness that characterizes much of *Howl*, Kerouac, in *On the Road*, celebrates a kind of divine madness; a joyful, liberating madness that lifts one out of the mundane into some other realm of reality. He lit up a whole generation with words like these, and he continues to do so for subsequent generations. As I point out elsewhere, Kerouac's divine madness, as celebrated in *On the Road* is also an overlay to the sadness and emptiness that are also a part of any journey of discovery.

Kerouac also imagined—however accurately is open to question—that he'd inherited his own brand of divine madness through his family lineage. Shortly after the publication of *On the Road* he published an essay called *The Origins of the Beat Generation*. Perhaps Kerouac was in a playful mood as he portrayed his paternal grandfather, Jean Baptiste Kerouac, as a progenitor of the Beat Generation:

It (the Beat Generation) goes back to the 1880s when my grandfather, Jean Baptiste Kerouac, used to go out on the porch in big thunderstorms and swing his kerosene lamp at the lightening and yell, "Go ahead, go, if you're more powerful than I am. Strike me and put the light out!" while the mother and the children cowered in the kitchen. And the light never went out.

This paternal grandfather of Kerouac's died in Nashua, New Hampshire, some 16 years before Jack was born. So Kerouac never met the man, but the stories about mad Jean Baptiste must have been a part of the Kerouac family lore. In his novel *Visions of Gerard* Kerouac also makes reference to his father Leo's "mad brothers and sisters who came from [Quebec] to the factories of the USA." So, from a grandfather who dared to match wits with God, to his "mad" uncles and aunts who struck out for new lives in a new land, Kerouac seemed to see himself as possessing a madness gene that that was inspiring his own work and bringing a sense of heightened life to the generation of which he was a part.

The spirituality the Beats sought, then, was one they believed was located somewhere within this divine/demonic madness matrix. What they were striving for, and reaching after, was the greater Yes that they believed was somewhere beyond the many No's they confronted. This striving, in fact, is the process that plays out in Ginsberg's *Howl*. As already noted, it is a harrowing journey Ginsberg takes you on in this particular piece of work, but one that ultimately leaves the reader with a Yes to Life.

Allen Ginsberg had yet another ongoing encounter with madness in the form of mental illness, however, that prevented him from ever romanticizing or glorifying such a condition. A serious kind of madness in Ginsberg's family stood in stark counterpoint to the joyful craziness that Kerouac celebrated in his family. Ginsberg was raised in a family whose dynamics were largely driven by the mental illness of his mother, Naomi. Allen, who was born in 1926, was the younger of the two sons of Louis and Naomi Ginsberg. Both of his parents were the offspring of Russian Jewish émigrés, and they settled in Patterson, New Jersey, where they raised Allen and Eugene Ginsberg. Louis was a high school English teacher, and a lyric poet of some local renown himself.

From the time Allen was a young boy his mother suffered increasingly intense episodes of depression, nervous breakdowns, and paranoid delusions. And while nudity itself is hardly a sign of mental illness, Naomi would frequently make a point of not wearing clothes around the Ginsberg household. When she went through some especially bad times, and could not be left alone, the teen-aged Allen stayed home with her. His father had school classes to teach, and his older brother, Eugene, was away in law school. Naomi eventually went through a series of institutionalizations at various mental hospitals in the New York and New Jersey area. Her last one was at the Pilgrim State Hospital on Long Island where she died in June of 1956. Ginsberg, by then, was 30 years old and living in Berkeley, California, when he received the news of his mother's death.

Two years later, still attempting to come to terms with the meaning of his mother's life and death and its impact upon his life, Allen Ginsberg would write his longest poem, *Kaddish*. By this time he was back living in New York City. A Kaddish is a Jewish prayer for the dead. It is impossible to read this poem without weeping in places as Ginsberg tells of his boyhood, his teen-age years, and his early adulthood with Naomi. In this piece he recounts a visit to see his mother after a two year hiatus:

Are you a spy?' I sat at the sour table, eyes filling with tears—'Who are you? Did Louis send you?—the wires' In her hair, as she beat on her head—'I'm not a bad girl—don't murder me!—I hear the ceiling—I raised two children—'

Two years since I'd been there—I started to cry—She started to cry—nurse broke up the meeting a moment—I went into the bathroom to hide against the toilet white walls...

I came back she yelled more—they led her away—'You're not Allen—' I watched her face—but she passed by me not looking—

Opened the door to the ward—she went thru without a glance back, quiet suddenly—I stared out—she looked old—the verge of the grave—'All the horror!'

So while Kerouac could revel in his "mad" grandfather and uncles and aunts, Ginsberg had seen another kind of madness altogether. A very real and hideous kind of madness destroyed his mother, even as he deeply needed her love, and wanted to give his love to her. Ginsberg, then, had to deal with madness on a number of levels: the severe mental illness that robbed his mother of her basic humanity; the psychological malady that was ascribed to him by the doctors at the New York Psychiatric Institute for his inability to live a so-called normal life; the cultural madness that he saw destroying "the best minds of my generation"; and finally a liberating, reach-for-starry-dynamo kind of madness that one needs to touch in order to breathe the true breath of life and achieve a certain kind of creative freedom. It was this latter kind of madness that Jack Kerouac saw in Ginsberg and wanted for himself, since Allen (as On the Road's Carlo Marx) is one of the "mad ones" to whom Kerouac refers and celebrates in that previously cited passage from On the Road.

The ways in which these various forms of madness played themselves out in the lives of Jack Kerouac and Allen Ginsberg have elements of deep irony, great triumph, and terrible tragedy. Ginsberg was well aware of how his mother's mental illness affected him. He attributed his paranoia about established authority, which he was generally able to keep in bounds, in part to the deadly and overwhelming paranoia of his mother. But Ginsberg refused to be defeated or overcome by the demonic madness he'd seen in his mother, or by the cultural madness he wrote of in *Howl* and in numerous other poems of his. He held his fear of demonic madness and his celebration of divine madness in some kind of spiritual balance, due in large measure, I feel, to the Buddhism he discovered in his early 20s, and that he studied and practiced for the rest of his life. His quest for the holy proved to be the stronger drive within him than a succumbing to demonic madness.

This spiritual balance allowed Ginsberg's artistic capabilities to flourish, and for his life—with all of its flaws and failings—to leave a positive mark on the society in which he lived. For all of the stark harshness found in much of Ginsberg's poetry—or maybe it's because of it—he became recognized as one of America's premier poets of the twentieth century. He was, as noted earlier, a Distinguished Professor at Brooklyn College in the latter part of his life. During these years he also gained recognition and respect as an accomplished photographer. Allen Ginsberg died two months shy of his seventy-first birthday in New York City on April 5, 1997, several weeks after a sudden onset of pancreatic cancer. World-wide, people mourned his death and celebrated his life.

Jack Kerouac, tragically, did not fare near as well. The madness he saw and celebrated in his family lineage had a pronounced element of alcoholism in it, to which Kerouac himself was far from immune. Kerouac also had to deal with the madness of instant fame and media celebrity-hood following the publication of *On the Road* in September of 1957, over seven years from the completion of the manuscript itself. Kerouac was, at heart, a sensitive and gentle soul who found himself the misunderstood and undeserving target of ridicule, contempt and fear by the self-appointed guardians of all that was supposedly right and proper about America, circa 1957. Ginsberg was able to walk through, and even revel in, the madness of fame once the Beats surfaced into the consciousness of mainstream America following the publications of *On the Road* and *Howl*. Kerouac, on the other hand, was destroyed by it.

Kerouac, too, sought spiritual solace and balance in Buddhism, which he first discovered in 1954, and which he attempted to practice in concert with his native Roman Catholicism. It worked for a time, but the balance didn't hold. Kerouac's eventual fate is tragically foreshadowed in his novel *Big Sur* where he describes an alcoholic breakdown he had while staying at Lawrence Ferlinghetti's cabin in the Big Sur area of the California coast in the late summer of 1960. As the seeds that the Beats planted in the 1950s came to flower in the 1960s, Kerouac retreated into alcoholic isolation and obscurity even as his novels continued to be published. At the time of his death in 1969 at age 47 he had published 18 novels and several works of poetry. His writings had also been widely translated for the European audience and readership that he had gained.

Given the markedly different paths their lives came to take, Allen Ginsberg and Jack Kerouac passionately loved life. They, each in their own way, had the artistic and poetic sensitivity and ability to hold that passionate love up to the society in which they lived. They each knew that in acting on their passion they had to risk demonic madness in order to celebrate divine madness. They each took their respective chances with that risk. They each lived with the results of the chances they took. In their glory and in their pain, they each touched the Holy. God bless and keep them both.

What is the legacy of these two when it comes to our own dealings with divine madness? I can best answer the question from a personal standpoint in the hope that my answer has some resonance beyond my life. I have chosen to live at a much lower level of risk than did Kerouac, Ginsberg, and their Beat Generation contemporaries. This happens to be true of most of the people I know, love, work with, and minister to. We hedge our bets with life. There's nothing wrong with that. There's even a lot that's right about it. Choosing a life of family, formal education, career, civic responsibility, etc. means cutting a deal with madness. The deal is that our own quests for divine madness and our own reachings for the Holy will take place within the overall boundaries of the lives we've chosen. That's the choice I've made and the deal I've cut—one I've long made my peace with.

Well…not entirely. There remains a part of me than never fully accepts the deal. I choose to regard this as a positive rather than as a negative. The part of me that won't completely close the deal is the same part that keeps me alive and growing. It's that part that lets me know that some madness is still worth risking, and that the Holy still awaits those who still take both seriously and joyously that simple admonition and promise of Jesus of Nazareth: "Seek and ye shall find."

As the search goes on what I keep before me are the lives and legacies of those who could not cut the deal. When Jack Kerouac put down his rifle on that naval base drill field and walked to the library, and when Allen Ginsberg declined the advice of the doctors at the Psychiatric Institute that he distance himself from his bohemian circle of friends and acquaintances and live a more conventional life, they were each indicating their unwillingness as well as their inability to cut the Madness Deal. As a result their lives, for better or for worse, took the courses they took. For that I thank them.

CHAPTER FIVE

William Burroughs and the Ugly Spirit as Muse

'I've created a Christmas Eve ritual just for myself. When the Christmas Eve service I lead is over, and I'm home and the rest of the family has gone to bed, I put on a CD recording of William S. Burroughs reading his short story, *A Junkie's Christmas*, written in 1954. He reads it in a flat, sardonic, mid-western twangy voice that Burroughs crafted into an art form. The best way to read Burroughs, I've come to discover, is to let the words on the page speak to you in WSB's voice and cadence. The best way to read Burroughs, in fact, is to let the page speak to you and hear what it says.

The central character in *A Junkie's Christmas* is Danny the Car Wiper. Against a background of softly playing Christmas Carols, Burroughs reads his story of Danny trying to score a drug fix in a virtually deserted New York City on Christmas Day. The story, by turns, is sad, pathetic, hilarious, disturbing, soulful, repulsive, and in the end, compassionate—the very adjectives that cover the range of Burroughs' writings.

In brief, Danny, after a few mis-attempts at lifting some goods he can fence, steals a suitcase from the stoop of an upper West Side brownstone, only to discover that it has a human arm in it. Unfazed, he dumps the arm and fences off the suitcase for a couple of bucks to one of his street compatriots. Then he scores a pill or two from a drunken doctor (a "croaker" in street/junkie language), uses the proceeds from the sale of the suitcase to rent himself a room where he cooks up the pills in a spoon, and prepares to inject himself. At this point the events of the story take a turn that result in Danny demonstrating, in his own way, the Spirit of the Season. I'll let the reader listen to the story for him/herself.

The character of Danny is loosely drawn from the person of Herbert Huncke, whom the reader has already met. Huncke introduced Burroughs to the drug and petty-criminal underworld of New York City in the mid-1940s. Burroughs, in turn, introduced Huncke to his circle of acquaintances who came together on New York's upper West Side at around that same time. Most of this circle came from middle-class to upper-middle-class families. Jack Kerouac, with his immigrant working class Lowell background, was the exception although he did come from a stable and closely-knit family.

Huncke became the Beat's doorman, as it were, to the underbelly of New York. If not for Burroughs they probably would have never met Huncke at all, and the course of Beat history might not have taken the direction it did. Burroughs poured Huncke's blended qualities of crook, hustler, and compassionate soul into the character of Danny the Car Wiper.

But Burroughs? What was a Harvard graduate, Class of 1936, with an impressive pedigree from one of the more upscale and better known families of St. Louis, Missouri—his grandfather invented the Burroughs Adding Machine—doing hanging out with a drug-dealer, con-man, petty thief, and street person from both the literal and figurative lower depths of New York City? The short answer is because he couldn't find any other place for himself. The longer answer is the incredibly fascinating, and at times utterly indecipherable, life of William Seward Burroughs. Even within the Beat circle, Burroughs was clearly an odd-ball; a genius, no doubt, but still the oddest among the odd.

Burroughs wasn't even around when the Beats finally came into public view. While the Beats were having their day in the sun in the late 1950s Burroughs was living the life of an expatriate in Tangiers, Paris, and London. He returned to the United States, on a more or less permanent basis, in 1973.

William's treatment of matters of religion and spirituality run from the caustic to the outrageous. One of his more oft-quoted lines is his well known piece of advice that "If you ever make a deal with a religious son of a bitch, make sure you get it in writing!" Burroughs' writings, however—some of which are more readable than others—are at base a challenge to his readers to determine what is ultimately real and trustworthy and what is not, which indeed is a challenge of the Spirit.

Burroughs was also one of the most trenchant satirists of his day, or of any day. Kerouac called him a modern-day Jonathan Swift. One of the challenges of reading satire is figuring out when you're being put on and when you're not; which, by extension, is one of the challenges of living itself. Burroughs voice, as I've said, often has such an undercurrent of sarcasm and extremely dry wit to it that the listener is not always quite sure of what s/he is hearing, even though the words themselves are perfectly clear.

You do not actually read Burroughs so much as you let yourself be washed over by his words, and then take a look at whatever might still be clinging to you. This is especially the case in his signature novel, *Naked Lunch*, which Burroughs claims to have written in its entirety while on heroin. Some people can handle these Burroughs baptisms and others cannot; which is to say that for some the Burroughs baptism is a way of salvation and for others it's a drenching they just plain don't want or need.

For Burroughs, the very act of writing was a spiritual undertaking in and of itself as he was attempting to overcome what he called an invasion of The Ugly Spirit. His most vivid encounter with this Ugly Spirit came about on a September afternoon in Mexico City in 1951. This is one of those stories that has taken on legendary dimensions in Beat Lore; and like most occurrences that expand into the realm of legend, an exact recounting of how the events unfolded is forever lost. But it doesn't matter. As is the case in most, if not all, religious traditions, legend and myth take on a greater reality and point to a greater meaning, than do the actual events behind them. If one treats, as I do, the Beat Movement as a religious phenomenon, with its own religious tradition then the same principle holds sway. Some of the legends of Beat Lore, for better and/or for worse, have taken on a greater reality than their historicity.

Bearing that in mind, this is the account/legend: In 1951 Burroughs was living in Mexico City with his common-law wife, Joan Vollmer Adams. She had been a part of the upper West Side bohemian circle in their earlier New York days. While his orientation was primarily homosexual, William and Joan shared a close and affectionate relationship and they even had a son together. Joan brought a daughter from an earlier marriage to their relationship. Like a number of persons who are both blessed and cursed with highly creative and strongly artistic inclinations, William and Joan lived in that danger zone where brilliance, creativity, and a penchant for self-destruction are intertwined. They had moved to Mexico City from New Orleans, Louisiana to avoid some pending drug possession charges Burroughs faced there.

Upon returning from an errand to have a knife sharpened William, Joan, and a few friends proceeded to do some heavy drinking in their Mexico City apartment. At one point, so the legend goes, after Bill had picked up a loaded pistol, Joan placed a glass on her head and said to her husband, "It's time for our William Tell act." She challenged Bill to shoot the glass off her head. The two of them had never actually concocted such a thing as a "William Tell act." It was a phrase Joan most likely came up with on the spur of the moment. But Burroughs apparently felt he had to rise to the challenge. So he took aim and fired. Instead of hitting the glass, however, the bullet went into Joan's forehead, and she died instantly. It was, by every account, an accidental shooting—horribly tragic and foolish as all hell, but still accidental—and Burroughs only had to deal with minor legal repercussions. He spent less than two weeks in a Mexico City jail. But the event largely defined his life from that point.

In 1985, with his literary career and reputation well established, Burroughs published his novel *Queer*, which he'd originally written right around the time of Joan's death. Nearly 35 years after the incident Burroughs felt he was finally ready to openly reflect on that horrible event in the novel's introduction:

> It was about three o'clock in the afternoon, a few days after I came back to Mexico City, [from a trip to Peru] and I decided to have (a) knife sharpened... as I walked down the street a feeling of loss and sadness that had weighed on me all day so I could hardly breathe intensified to such an extent that I found tears streaming down my face. "What on earth is wrong?" I wondered...
>
> I have constrained myself to remember the day of Joan's death, the overwhelming feeling of doom and loss...
>
> I am forced to the appalling conclusion that I would never have become a writer except for Joan's death, and to a realization of the extent

to which this event has motivated and formulated my writing. I live with the constant threat of possession, and the constant need to escape from possession, from Control. The death of Joan brought me into contact with the invader, the Ugly Spirit, and maneuvered me in to a life-long struggle, in which I have no choice except to write my way out.

What these sentiments strongly suggest to me is that much of the Burroughs *oeuvre* is an exorcism, and to read him is to be invited to witness the author being his own exorcist. They also indicate that the Ugly Spirit became Burroughs' life-long Muse.

The odyssey of William S. Burroughs is one of the most fascinating and confounding ones in American literary history. Of all the major Beat writers Burroughs, far and away, came from the most privileged background. His grandfather, as noted, invented and held the patent for the Burroughs Adding Machine, and founded the Burroughs Adding Machine Corporation. (So, naturally, Burroughs eventually published a collection of essays called, *The Adding Machine*.) But William's father, Mortimer Burroughs, sold his inherited share of stock in the Burroughs Corporation to help his family weather the Depression; so neither he, nor his family, ever reaped any of the huge dividends the Corporation later produced. Still, they fared well enough. William was a beneficiary of a small family trust fund from his Harvard days on which provided him with a subsistence level of living—when he wasn't using it as drug money.

Like Allen Ginsberg, Burroughs was the younger of two sons. As in the Ginsberg family, there was a "good" older brother and a "misfit" younger brother. Ginsberg's older brother was a lawyer. Mortimer Burroughs, Jr., William's brother, lived most of his life in St. Louis as a solid citizen, working for many years as a draftsman for the General Electric Company prior to his retirement. Mortimer, Jr. died in 1983, pre-deceasing his misfit younger brother by almost 15 years. How two individuals, close in age, with the same set of parents, raised in the same environment, and given the same head-starts in life, can have their lives go in such radically divergent directions is yet another of life's many unsolved mysteries.

Burroughs' struggles of the soul and spirit can perhaps be traced in part to some of his earliest years when he heard descriptive references made about him by adults in his company that let him know that he was not exactly, well, normal. The references included phrases like "unwholesome" and "walking corpse" and "sheep killing dog." The fact that Burroughs later recalled and recounted such characterizations in his writings gives a good indication of the impact they had on him. With the possible exception of the last few years of his life, which he spent with his companion, secretary, and business manager James Grauerholz in Lawrence, Kansas, I don't know if Burroughs ever felt that he truly belonged anywhere or with anyone. There was a part of him, it seems, that actually bought into, and internalized, some of the characterizations ascribed to him in his adolescence. And while he cultivated and maintained, at various times in his life, some very intense and intimate friendships—nearly all of them with males—William also seems to have lived with a pronounced sense of alienation from his surroundings.

In one of his essays Burroughs quipped: "After one look at this planet any visitor from outer space would say, 'I WANT TO SEE THE *MANAGER*.'" With that quip Burroughs described, in large measure, his own stance between himself and the world—that of a visitor from some other planet demanding to know who (Who?) is in charge. Along with an attempt to exorcise the Ugly Spirit, Burroughs work is also an ongoing demand to "see the Manager."

Could such a life, and such a life stance, be those of a spirit guide? While bits and pieces of William's life have already been revealed I'll offer a tiny, nut-shell version of the Burroughs odyssey here. His early years were lived as a child of privilege in St. Louis. He attended private schools, including one in Los Alamos, New Mexico, before going to Harvard in 1932. He graduated from Harvard in 1936. From that point on, until the latter years of his life, Burroughs was a wanderer. During the seven years following his graduation from Harvard he spent some time in Europe where he witnessed the rise of Nazism, did a brief hitch in the Army, and then bounced around between St. Louis, Boston, and Chicago. In 1943 he moved to New York where he became a part of the early Beat circle.

While Burroughs had little aspiration to be a writer at this point, his improvisation of oral routines within his circle of associates foreshadowed some of the completely out-there elements of his later writings. In New York he also began the cultivation of his fascination with the carny underworld of small time outlaws, whores, and drug dealers and users. This led to an ongoing struggle with drug addiction, from which he would occasionally free himself, only to fall into it again.

He quit the New York scene after a few years, first to try his hand at farming in east Texas, and then to live in New Orleans with Joan. Their son, William, Jr. was born while they were in Texas, and Billy Burroughs spent most of his early years with his Burroughs grandparents. From 1949 to 1953 Burroughs lived in Mexico City, during which time he made a trip to South America in search of the drug *yage*, an aphrodisiac and hallucinogen. Then, from 1953 to 1973 Burroughs lived the life of an expatriate, first in Tangiers and then alternating between London and Paris. During this period he made a few brief return visits to the United States. While in Tangiers he wrote his major work, *Naked Lunch.* His only previously published work at that time was *Junky*, a completely unvarnished look at the drug world and the realities of drug addiction.

In 1973 New York became his base of operation as his literary fame (or infamy) began to grow. In 1980, under the urging and direction of James Grauerholz, Burroughs returned to the Midwest to live in James' home state of Kansas, and in the University town of Lawrence. Here he purchased his only permanent residential home. In Lawrence he went into the final phase of his writing, and saw some of the rewards and returns of his prolific writing career, including his induction into the American Academy and Institute of Arts and Letters in 1982. William Seward Burroughs died on August 2, 1997, at the age of 83, four months after the death of his near life-long literary companion and soul-mate, Allen Ginsberg.

As was the case with Ginsberg's *Howl, Naked Lunch* also had to go through the rite-of-passage of an obscenity trial before it could be considered fit to read by thinking adults. It was a piece of testimony offered by Norman Mailer during that trial that offers a key, I feel, to approaching Burroughs as a religious writer and spirit guide. Norman Mailer said from the stand:

> William Burroughs is in my opinion—whatever his conscious inten-
> tion may be—a religious writer. There is a sense in *Naked Lunch* of the
> destruction of the soul, which is more intense than any I have encoun-
> tered in any other modern novel. It is a vision of how mankind would
> act if man was totally divorced from eternity. What gives this vision a
> machine-gun-edged clarity is an utter lack of sentimentality...Burroughs

avoids even the possibility of sentimentality by attaching a stringent, mordant vocabulary to a series of precise and horrific events, a species of gallows humor which is a defeated man's last pride, the pride that he has, at least, not lost his bitterness.

"A vision of how mankind (*sic*) would act if man was totally divorced from eternity." By eternity I do not believe Mailer means time—as we understand time—going on forever. Rather, life divorced from any sense of Eternity means life being lived completely apart from some larger, wholistic sense of what life is finally about, that is, life apart from any ultimate meaning or purpose. Building on Mailer's words, the theologian Paul Tillich held that the word "God" refers to that which gives Life its Ultimate Meaning and Purpose above and beyond the many penultimate meanings—both for good and for ill—that we build our lives around. Couple Tillich's understanding of God with something Burroughs said in the last major interview he granted before his death for *Rolling Stone* magazine: "I believe in God and always have. *I don't think anyone could read my books and think otherwise*" (emphasis added).

To many of Burroughs' readers that is a very startling assertion. Not many people, I would venture to say, read Burroughs' books and come away believing in God, much less convinced of Burroughs' belief in God—certainly not God in any traditionally theistic sense. But if one puts Burroughs' *Rolling Stone's* "profession of faith" in conversation both with Mailer's *Naked Lunch* testimony, and with Tillich's theology, a certain sensibility begins to emerge.

Much of Burroughs work is about the absence of God; not God in any authoritarian or controlling sense since Burroughs' work is also a life-long railing against practically all forms of authority and control, but the absence of God in the sense of the absence of any Transcendent Meaning to Life Itself. But, since Burroughs said he'd always believed in God, (and he did say he meant his words to be taken literally) then he must have been holding out for at least the possibility of Transcendent Meaning, even as he took his readers on a journey through a harrowing, frightening, revolting—and at times insanely hilarious—world where, in Mailer's apt words, the reader witnesses "the destruction of the soul."

For Burroughs such destruction had to precede the construction of any viable philosophy of life. Perhaps his life-long battle with the Ugly Spirit was done in the hope—consciously held on his part or not—of eventually embracing the Spirit of Life Itself. As stated earlier, two of the major themes in Burroughs' work have to do with 1) the trustworthiness of the senses, that is, how do we really *know* what it is we are seeing, hearing, thinking, experiencing, etc; and 2) who is controlling what when it comes to what we *do* know—or *think* we know. These are spiritual issues in the sense that they have to be worked through before one can even begin to apprehend any Eternal dimension to life. Sitting down to a Naked Lunch means—as Burroughs himself suggested—being willing to look closely, and at times even painfully, at all that we're being asked to swallow while it is right there on the end of a fork.

Naked Lunch is a deliberate assault on the senses. It is somewhat akin to the physical tests of endurance that prospective astronauts endure in order to see if they can handle the challenges of space travel. The challenge for the reader of *Naked Lunch*, as with many of Burroughs's works, is: Can one's senses take that kind of pounding and then see clearly enough to be on a meaningful life journey with a markedly clearer perception.

This is the same challenge and test Burroughs put forth with his "cut-up" style of writing. A cut-up text was created by slicing up a page, or pages, of print—usually in fourths—and then rearranging the pieces to form a new text. With this approach Burroughs attempted to accomplish with the printed word on a page of text what abstract and surrealistic artists do with the painted image on a canvas, that is to say, to first de-range the senses when it comes to how what we call conventional reality is perceived, in order that other dimensions of reality and meaning might be at least apprehended, even if they cannot be fully comprehended. Certain psychedelic drugs are also supposed to accomplish this end. This is not, however, a route I have chosen to take.

Burroughs other predominant theme is Control, and who or what controls how we know what we know and believe what we believe. One of his stock, and oft-recurring characters in his work is Dr. Benway, a deranged physician (i.e. one who holds matters of life and death in his hands) who is given to continually insisting that "everything is under control" when, in fact, everything is falling apart at the seams. Example: at one of his New York nightclub appearances in the early 80's William signed off with this tag line: "Doctor Benway couldn't be here tonight, but he asked me to give you the message that everything is under control...in Jonestown." Some of Burroughs best and most trenchant humor comes through in his Dr. Benway routines.

In this "who is controlling what" vein Burroughs devotes a good deal of his thought and writing to his concern for the integrity of language and of the Word. As a writer, of course, he recognized the indispensable nature of language and how the use of language is basic to our humanity. He would probably agree with the idea, as stated in the first verse of the New Testament Gospel of John, "In the beginning was the Word;" meaning that the development of written language was and is an essential element of the human story itself. But the demonic side of this verse is that the Word is also a Virus. The Word is also an instrument of thought control and manipulation in the hands of the powerful, and has been so ever since "The Beginning."

The language we use goes a long way in determining our sense of reality, and those who control and dictate the language go a long way in determining how we perceive and relate to our world and universe. For Burroughs his outlandish routines, his over-the-top provocative and shocking imagery, and his cut-ups were his antibiotics for the Word Virus.

If William were with us today I am quite sure he would offer the term Patriot Act as Exhibit A for the Word Virus. In order to be regarded as a patriot one must adhere to the word and letter of the Patriot Act. Not to do so is to be an Enemy of the State, and to set oneself in the dangerous position of being the enemy of the forces of Control. I can just picture William Burroughs reading the Patriot Act and giving that trademark tight-lipped grin of his and slowly nodding his head up and down.

So I include William S. Burroughs in my gallery of Beat Spirit Guides even though just reading him can be a taxing and exacting experience. I have to take Burroughs in measured doses. I'd much rather cruise along with Kerouac in *On the Road* or *The Dharma Bums* than have my senses jarred to their foundation by *Naked Lunch* or *The Ticket That Exploded*. But this jarring of the senses is the essential point when it comes to Burroughs. He always keeps before his readers the challenge of determining the trustworthiness of one's perceptions and of one's concept of reality, when it comes to seeking out meaning, direction, and purpose in life and living, which is what the spiritual journey is finally all about. Whoever or Whatever Burroughs took God to be, he knew that one did not gain the Blessing of the Holy Spirit without first facing down the Ugly Spirit.

According to the Old Testament myth, Jacob had to wrestle all night with an Angel/Demon—and be deeply wounded in the course of his wrestling—before he received the Blessing of Yahweh. And in the Beat Scripture it is William Burroughs, who had a "life long struggle with the Ugly Spirit," in which he had no choice but to "write my way out," who finally attained some measure of peace in his final years. I cannot improve upon the words of James Grauerholz as he summed up the life of his beloved friend and companion after William's death at the conclusion of a posthumous release of a Burrough's anthology called *Word Virus* (Grove Press, 1998):

> Outcast from society, and moreover self-exiled…William Seward Burroughs created himself. Homosexual, insecure, wounded by childhood mistreatment, haunted by an Ugly Spirit, he summoned every force whose name he knew to guide him on his path toward "the only goal worth striving for": immortality. And as his final writings show, on the long, hard journey to his own well-assured literary immortality, Burroughs finally glimpsed the meaning of human life: compassion for all life's endless suffering, and for its inexorable end.

To these words of Mr. Grauerholz I can only add: Blessed be, William. Blessed be.

Epilogue: I've finished this chapter while on sabbatical at a theological school in the Hyde Park section of Chicago. From the window of my third floor apartment I can look out over the screen of my laptop and see the tops of the buildings of the University of Chicago. This gives me a view of a few slices of Burroughs' life. It was here in 1939 that William enrolled in a seminar led by Count Alfred Korzybski on general semantics and theories of language, and so began his explorations into the workings of the Word. When, in 1958, the University of Chicago's *Chicago Review* refused to publish excerpts from *Naked Lunch*, the editor of the *Review* resigned in protest and started an alternative magazine called *Big Table* so that Burroughs' work would get an airing. If I look over towards the city's North Side I can see the general area where, in the summer of 1942, Burroughs had a job as an insect exterminator for the A.J. Cohen Company. We may have lost you several years ago, Mr. Burroughs, but looking through this window I know you're out there somewhere!

CHAPTER SIX

The West Coast Beats—Buddhists Before Buddhism Was Cool

One bright summer New England morning my son headed out the door saying he was on his way to Portsmouth, New Hampshire, about an hour's drive from our home, to go on a whale watch. I think it was mostly his girlfriend's idea, but he was willing to oblige. By all accounts they had a good time, and, no doubt, helped out Portsmouth's summer tourist economy. In many American coastal towns and cities, where there are offshore pods of whales nearby, whale watches have become something of a growth industry. Get yourself a boat and a Whale Watch sign and you're in business.

If we go back about a century and a half, the growth industry around whales was whale slaughters. In those Melvillean days, killing whales at least served an economic and utilitarian purpose, as whale blubber and whale oil were basic staples in many nineteenth-century homes. By the mid-twentieth-century, however, those staples were replaced by synthetic substitutes. But whale slaughters, apparently, were still ongoing. In April, 1954, a short and rather matter-of-fact article ran in *Time* magazine about how killer whales—referred to in the article as "savage sea cannibals"—were destroying the nets of fishermen in the seas off Greenland and Iceland. The story continued:

> (The) Icelandic government appealed to the United States, which
> has thousands of men stationed at a lonely NATO airbase on the sub

artic island. Seventy-nine armed GIs responded with enthusiasm. Armed with rifles and machine guns one posse of Americans climbed into four small boats and in one morning wiped out a pack of 100 killers.

Among those reading this account was a twenty-one year old San Francisco poet named Michael McClure. His revulsion at this story, presented in the mainstream media as a more or less innocuous happening, moved him to write a poem titled *For the Death of 100 Whales*. In this poem he vents his anger and revulsion at the slaughter of these creatures, portraying their treatment as a violation of the Sacred. These are its final two verses:

> Turned and twisted
> (Goya!)
> Flung blood and sperm.
> Incense.
> Gnashed at their tails and brothers,
> Cursed Christ of mammals,
> Snapped at the sun,
> Ran for the sea's floor.
>
> Goya! Goya!
> Oh Lawrence
> No angels dance those bridgtes.
> OH GUN! OH BOW!
> There are no churches in the waves,
> No holiness,
> No passages or crossings
> From the beasts' wet shore.

I don't know that the young Mr. McClure had even seen a whale at that point in his life. He had just that year (1954) moved to San Francisco from his native state of Kansas, where whale sightings are...well, pretty rare. But McClure knew a hideous wrong had been committed, whale sightings or not. It was a wrong that called out for the response of a poet, and he answered the call. On the same night, and in the same locale, where Allen Ginsberg read *Howl* for the first time, McClure read *For the Death of 100 Whales*.

The night was October 7, 1955 and the locale was a loft on San Francisco's

Fillmore Avenue, known at that time as the Six Gallery. The poetry reading featured a constellation of young Bay Area poets and writers who had been holding periodic gatherings, and sharing their work, at the home of essayist, commentator, and poet Kenneth Rexroth. Being one generation older than those gathered around him, Rexroth was regarded as the elder statesman of the group, so it was fitting that he served as the host of this event. Allen Ginsberg, who had arrived in the Bay Area over a year earlier, organized and promoted the event. Among those reading, in addition to Ginsberg and McClure were Gary Snyder, and Philip Whalen. Philip Lamantia also read, but from another fellow poet's work. Jack Kerouac attended but did not read. Neal Cassady and his girlfriend, Natalie Jackson, were also there. A fictionalized, but reasonably accurate, account of this gathering can be found in an early chapter of Kerouac's *The Dharma Bums*. A more historically detailed account of the Six Gallery reading can be found in John Suiter's *Poets on the Peaks* (Counterpoint, 2002).

So-called "beginning of an era" dates are usually arbitrary and far from precise, but the date of this poetry reading serves as a good marker to signal the origins of the West Coast, or San Francisco Bay Area, version of the Beat movement. The Six Gallery event was, in a matter of speaking, the coming out party for the West Coast Beats. About ten years earlier, as we have seen, Kerouac, Ginsberg, Burroughs, Lucien Carr, Joan Adams, Edie Parker, and Herbert Huncke found one another on New York City's upper West Side and in Greenwich Village. In similar fashion, in 1954-55 another group of aspiring poets and young bohemians on the other end of the country began finding one another in and around San Francisco and Berkeley.

Although originally an East Coast guy, Allen Ginsberg became an integral part of both scenes. In San Francisco, in 1955, he met his life-long companion and lover, Peter Orlovsky. Jack Kerouac occasionally visited this West Coast confluence, and Gregory Corso, while New York City based, also showed up from time to time. Granting that far more than three persons played significant roles in both locations, the East and West Coast Beat Scenes each did have their own "trinity." In the East it was Kerouac, Ginsberg, and Burroughs; in the West it was Gary Snyder, Michael McClure, and Lawrence Ferlinghetti. Philip Whalen also belongs with that trio, but then you'd have a four-person trinity, and that would upset this whole East

Coast/West Coast balancing thing I'm trying to do!

My attempts at trinitarian balance aside, one distinguishing mark of the West Coast Beats was their earth-based, earth-centered spirituality. This spiritual stance was not at odds with anything the East Coast Beats expressed, but it received considerably more emphasis in the West. Earth-centered spirituality, in broadly defined terms, means that one's sense of the sacred is derived from cultivating a relationship with the Earth, and with all of Creation, rather than by standing apart from Creation. This stance seeks one's rightful place within the interdependent Web of Existence rather than assuming, or attempting, mastery over that Web. This stance seeks ways of living in a rightful relationship with all of Life Itself without assuming the innate superiority of human life over all others. Persons who resonate with this kind of earth-based spirituality may differ over what the rightful place for human beings is within the Web of Life, or with what right relationship actually means when it comes to their day-to-day living. But their emphasis is upon living with some meaningful level of harmony with the Earth and its creatures, rather than assuming one's human status automatically grants mastery, or dominion, over the Earth and its creatures.

This assumption of innate human superiority made it OK in 1954 for a contingent of armed soldiers to machine-gun one hundred whales to death, since they were, after all, getting in the way of a human enterprise like fishing. The *Time* article called the giant creatures of the sea "killer whales" because they were killing and eating other creatures of the sea. That they were "killer whales" became an implied justification that it was OK for human beings to retaliate. What did the author of this article think the Icelandic fishermen, whose nets were being torn up by the whales, were doing with the fish they were hauling up in their nets? Taking them home for pets?

The point is not that the Icelandic fishermen were bad people doing bad things by pulling fish out of the ocean for people to buy and eat. Theirs was an honorable livelihood, given the overall context of their lives. The point is that both the fishermen and the whales were doing the same basic and essential thing, killing other life forms in order that each species could live. Life feeds on life, after all. The question, the admittedly tough, no-easy-answer question of how to best let that process go forward when it came to human beings on the one hand and whales on the other, never even got onto the radar screen, or into the consciousness, of those involved in this particular incident, including the writer who reported it. Mindless reaction just said kill the whales. It took the consciousness of a young poet out of Kansas to at least raise the question, and to pose it to a gathering of San Francisco poets.

This consciousness grew out of a spiritual sense of connection with all of Life Itself. The kind of awareness expressed by Michael McClure, and his poetic comrades of the time, was largely alien in 1955 because the dominant religions of the culture, Christianity and Judaism, assumed a self/world or self/universe stance that largely militated against such awareness. The core myth of both the Christian and Judaic faiths is that of the human creature—in the archetypal forms of Adam and Eve—being brought forth by the Creator as the crowning act of creation itself, and then told to "have dominion over the earth." And if it is God who says to have dominion, then who's to argue with that?

It is far from necessary to take this myth literally in order to live out its implications. The implication is that the Earth, and all it contains, are at the disposal of human beings to use as we see fit. Granted there's an element of earthly stewardship implied here in that we need to keep the Earth in some reasonably decent shape so we can continue to be served by it. But this is akin to a slave master recognizing the wisdom of keeping his slaves reasonably healthy and content so he can continue to extract the maximum benefit from them. A slave master, however, cannot allow himself to see any inherent, much less egalitarian, relationship with his slaves, since to do so would be to question the very rightness of the bondage itself. He cannot allow himself to think about what changing the very nature of the dominion assumed within the master/slave relationship would mean.

In fairness I will grant that significant elements within both the Christian and Judaic communions have come to recognize the serious harm and danger to this planet that the "have dominion" myth has brought on. Some make serious efforts to reinterpret this myth in such a way that calls for a genuine and nurturing partnership between humans and the earth. The National Association of Evangelicals, no less, has drafted a resolution warning of the effects of global warming. More power to them, I say.

But as far back as the 1950s, the West Coast Beats were cultivating a spirituality grounded in a relationship with the earth, and the processes of nature, rather than with a transcendent and all-powerful Supreme Being. While not all of them were active, practicing Buddhists their various modes of spirituality had, and have, a high level of resonance and compatibility with Buddhism. As Buddhist scholar Gary Gach puts it, "The spiritual and the natural are indivisible. As Buddhists have been saying for thousands of years, Buddha's body can be seen in the colors of the mountains; in the sound of the water, we can hear Buddha's voice." [Gary Gach. *The Complete Idiot's Guide to Buddhism*. Alpha Press, 2002.]

Among the West Coast Beats, an individual whose life and writings especially embody Gary Gach's words, and whose life provides a striking example of the confluence of Buddhism, Beatness, and Earth-based spirituality is another Gary—the poet and deep ecologist, Gary Snyder. Snyder was 28 years old when he was introduced as "Japhy Ryder" in Kerouac's *The Dharma Bums*, one of Kerouac's better works and one that was written to catch the wave of popularity generated by *On the Road*. But Kerouac was not content to simply write a pot-boiler to please the publishers who had been ignoring him for years. *The Dharma Bums* is a wonderful book that captures well the spirit of the San Francisco Renaissance. Kerouac captures Snyder pretty well at that point also. As was the case, however, with Dean Moriarty/Neal Cassady, there is vastly more to Gary Snyder than that of a character in a novel, however well written.

The story of Snyder's amazing life, which as of this writing is still going strong, is well beyond the scope of a single chapter in this book. A short synopsis will have to suffice. Gary Snyder grew up in rural Washington State and spent some of his early summers backpacking in its mountains, including a trip to the top of Mt. Saint Helens at age 15. While an undergraduate at Reed College in Portland, Oregon he met Philip Whalen, and the two became Buddhist buddies for life. Also at this time in his life Snyder began a series of jobs with the United States Park Service and Forest Service as a fire lookout on some of the higher peaks in the northern Cascades. He also worked with loggers in various capacities and got a good taste of that rough-and-tumble kind of life. Some of his earliest poems come from this period.

In an indication of the political lunacy of that time, in 1954 Snyder was blacklisted by the United States Park Service for being a member of a so-called subversive organization. Six years earlier, at age eighteen, while on a brief trip to New York City in the summer of 1948, Gary had joined the National Union of Marine Cooks and Stewards in order to get a job on a Caribbean-bound freighter. As the McCarthy Era gained momentum, this Union was named as one of numerous alleged Communist front organizations. The fact that Snyder's name was on an old membership list for this Union was enough to put him on the U.S. Government's shit-list.

For a beautifully written, and illustrated, account of Snyder's—as well as Jack Kerouac's and Philip Whalen's—experiences as fire lookouts in the Pacific Northwest in the early-to-mid-1950s, I highly recommend John Suiter's *Poets on the Peaks* (Counterpoint, 2002).

By 1954 Snyder was well into his Zen Buddhist studies and practiced in earnest at the University of California at Berkeley. All the while he continued to write his poems, many of which celebrated our earthly creature qualities. From 1956 to 1968 he alternated between living on the West Coast and in Japan, with much of his time in Japan spent at a Zen temple in Kyoto. In 1969 he moved back to the United States, more or less permanently.

In 1972 Snyder made his mark on the poetic community by winning the Pulitzer Prize for Poetry for his collection titled *Turtle Island*. As he explains in the book's introduction the term Turtle Island is derived from various American Indian mythologies as the name for the North American continent itself. Of the poems in this work Snyder says they "speak of place, and the energy-pathways that sustain life. Each living being is a swirl in the flow, a formal turbulence, a 'song.' The land, the planet itself, is also a living being—at another pace." By 1972 the cultural consciousness had shifted just enough from its place some 20 years earlier so that these words, and the poems that reflected them, could be heard. Continuing on his path of poet and global environmentalist, Snyder joined the faculty of the University of California at Davis, a position from which he is now retired. A comprehensive collection of his life-long work, *The Gary Snyder Reader* (Counterpoint) was published in 1999.

Snyder's comment in the *Turtle Island* introduction about the very land and planet as a living being has gained increasing currency since he first put it forth over 30 years ago. This kind of perspective hearkens back to some of the earliest religious practices on this planet which treated Nature itself as alive, as a living organism, with human beings as participants in its aliveness. One term for this kind of understanding of nature and persons is animism. A pejorative term which an increasingly powerful European Christian Church applied to such a stance was paganism. Pagan (In Latin, *paganus*) simply means country dweller. In the eyes of the Church, a pagan was one who lived so far from the emerging urbanized areas of Europe that s/he had not yet been properly and rightfully Christianized. The term heathen is of similar derivation. It comes from the British Isles and from roughly the same time period. A heathen was one who lived out on the rural heaths of Britain where, again, the influence of the Church had not yet reached. Converting the pagans and heathens meant, among numerous other things, weaning them off the idea that they were part of a larger, living organism called Earth, or Universe, or Nature, to the idea or belief that the Earth had been created by the Christian God, and was an entity over which human beings ruled or had dominion.

One term for the effort, on the part of some, to re-capture or reclaim an awareness of a pre-Christian self/earth/universe relationship is neo-paganism. Much of Snyder's poetry has a neo-pagan flavor to it. In a small bit of correspondence between Mr. Snyder and myself I mentioned that some people I know—including some in my congregation who consider themselves neo-pagans—find a very sympathetic and understanding voice in much of his poetry. While granting that much of his writing does cater to such a perspective, Snyder went on to say, "I'm not a neo-pagan, but rather an old style Ch'an Buddhist." Ch'an is the Chinese term for Zen—as in Zen Buddhism.

There is no contradiction, however, between Zen Buddhism and neo-paganism as I've just briefly described it. Zen, in its most literal sense means meditation; meditation, in this case, as a way of being fully present in the present, and in a timeless state. I am not a practitioner of Zen. But I regard a "Zen moment" as a time when one is so fully focused on the Now that there are no distractions—only the immediate awareness that one is Here and Now. Cultivating this kind of awareness has been the sustaining constant in Gary Snyder's life. Also, by good indication, this kind of Zen awareness has given Snyder his sense of relatedness with all of Being. This sense is conveyed in much of his earth-based and earth-centered poetry. Many of his poems have a playful, whimsical quality as the writer delights in his relationship with the living being of which he is also a part. Snyder's playfulness in his poetry also shows his readers a person who is very serious about what he is saying and doing, without taking himself all that seriously at all.

The reader will have to take his/her own walk with Gary Snyder by way of his poetry. I can offer only a few steps here. In *It Pleases*, written in Washington, D.C., in November of 1973, our world of seemingly important events is shrugged at by a world beyond them; and a world that also contains them:

Far above the dome
Of the capitol—
      It's true!
A large bird soars
Against a white cloud,
Wings arched
Sailing easy in this
humid Southern sun-burned
        breeze—
      the dark-suited policeman
      watches tourist cars—

And the center,
The center of power is nothing!
Nothing here.
Old white stone domes
Strangely quiet people,

Earth-sky-bird patterns
      Idly interlacing

The world does what it pleases.

Snyder's poem/meditation *Prayer for the Great Family*, which he adapts from a Mohawk prayer, is one that could be used in a worship service, with its litany-like quality:

Gratitude to Mother Earth, sailing through night and day—
    and to her soil: rich, rare, and sweet

in our minds so be it.

Gratitude to Plants, the sun-facing light-changing leaf
    and fine root-hairs; standing still through wind
    and rain; their dance is in the flowing spiral grain
    in our minds so be it.

Gratitude to Air, bearing the soaring Swift and the silent
    Owl at dawn. Breath of our song
    clear spirit breeze
    in our minds so be it.

Gratitude to Wild Beings, our brothers, teaching secrets,
    freedoms, and ways; who share with us their milk;
    self-complete, brave, and aware.
    in our minds so be it.

Gratitude to Water: clouds, lakes, rivers glaciers;
    holding or releasing; streaming through all
    our bodies salty seas
    in our minds so be it.

Gratitude to the Sun: blinding pulsing light through
    trunks of trees, through mists, warming caves where
    bears and snakes sleep—he who wakes us—
    in our minds so be it.

Gratitude to the Great Sky
    who holds billions of stars—and goes yet beyond that—
    beyond all powers, and thoughts
    and yet is within us—
    Grandfather Space.
    The Mind is his Wife

    so be it.

With his now 75 years of living (2005) on Turtle Island, Gary Snyder has shown to many the sacredness of life, both on Turtle Island and on our island planet itself. Through his many interactions with folk like Jack Kerouac, Allen Ginsberg, Michael McClure, Lawrence Ferlinghetti, Gregory Corso, and a host of others, he helped bring to the Beat Generation writers a way of sensing and touching the essential holiness of life they were seeking. While not all of them followed Snyder's Buddhist path in the manner that he did, their ties to him as he followed that path connected Beat to Beatitude.

As noted earlier, Snyder was part of a larger circle of like-minded poets and artists who began finding one another in the San Francisco area in the early 1950s. Two members of this circle, Philip Whalen and Lew Welch, were fellow students of Snyder's at Reed College. Phil Whalen, who, like Snyder, worked for several summers as a fire lookout in the Northwest Cascades, also became a serious student and practitioner of Zen Buddhism. Whalen was eventually ordained as a Zen monk, and in 1991 became an abbot at the Hartford Street Zen Center in San Francisco. He died in June of 2002. Philip Whalen's down to earth kindness is portrayed through the character of Ben Fagan in Kerouac's *Big Sur*. Fagan/Whalen is the patient friend who tries in vain to save Kerouac from himself.

Lew Welch, who also fares rather prominently in *Big Sur*, did not fare nearly as well as Whalen or Snyder. A gifted and published poet in his own right, he battled demons of alcoholism and depression. In May, 1971, during a visit with Gary Snyder in California's Nevada County, he went into the woods with a gun, and disappeared. While his body has never been found, the presumption is that he committed suicide. In addition to his poetry, Welch, in his book *Trip Trap*, tells a delightful tale of a cross-country jaunt with Kerouac and Albert Saijo in Welch's jeep following Kerouac's appearance on the Steve Allen Show in the fall of 1959.

During the time of the events in Kerouac's *Big Sur*—late summer, 1960—the woman in Welch's life was Lenore Kandel. Her earthy celebration of sexuality in *The Love Book* was enough to merit her still another Beat-inspired obscenity trial. Whether the trial was brought on by the book itself, or by the idea that women of that era were not supposed to be so forthrightly erotic, is a good question. After dropping out of sight in the early 1970s following a serious motorcycle accident, Ms. Kandel has recently resurfaced.

Along with Snyder, the other key figure in this San Francisco circle was, and is, the still-going-strong Lawrence Ferlinghetti. More fully discussed in a later chapter, Ferlinghetti at least needs to be mentioned here. While he has not engaged in a Buddhist practice to the extent that Snyder has, Ferlinghetti has long been Buddhist-friendly. Shortly after the FBI attack on the Branch Davidian compound in Waco, Texas, he wrote a poem called *A Buddha in the Woodpile*. The gist of the poem is that brute force was assumed to be the primary means of dealing with the Davidians with few alternative methods seriously pursued:

> If only in the land of Sam Houston...
> one had comprehended
> one single syllable
> of the Gautama Buddha
> of the young Siddhartha
> one single whisper of
> Gandhi's spinning wheel...
> Then that sick cult and its children
> might still be breathing...

It is a frustrating irony that at the same time and place where Beat was being seriously and joyfully and playfully pursued as meaning Beatific, the snide appellation "beatnik" was coined—as noted in Chapter One—by Herb Caen of the *San Francisco Chronicle*. Some of the Beats, in turn, appropriated the term for themselves in the time-honored manner of taking a negative characterization and wearing it as a badge of honor. This is what gay and lesbian persons have now done with the term "queer." Often times the best thing to do with a put-down label is to make it a badge and wear it.

With the West Coast Beats bringing Buddhism to Beatness, I can see yet another meaning of the term. Beat can also mean to align oneself with the Beat of Life and with the Beat of the Universe. I do not follow a Buddhist practice in any disciplined way—I lack the discipline, quite literally, to sit still for it. Perhaps I shall yet learn to do so, to the greater enrichment of my life, I'm sure.

But Buddhist or not, in the lives and writings of persons like Gary Snyder, Michael McClure, and Philip Whalen, those on a spiritual path can find yet another set of guides. We each and all live and move and have our beings in a great Chain of Life that began well before we were born, or before the first humans emerged. And that Chain will very likely continue well after Earth's last human being has taken a last breath. For the briefest of moments, in the overall span of this Chain, we're given a life to live and many choices as to how to live it. One of the most important of those choices we make is the choice to live, as best we can, in accordance with the Rhythm and Beat of Life that ultimately nurtures and sustains us.

The West Coast Beats, like their East Coast counterparts, may have been non-conformists in the society in which they lived. But they sought a greater kind of conformity, an Ultimate Conformity, if you will. They sought a Conformity with All That Is—and tried to show us that Way as well. For this we offer them our thanks.

CHAPTER SEVEN

"We Are Not Our Skin of Grime"
A Meditation on Allen Ginsberg's
Sunflower Sutra

n epiphany, by one definition, is an appearance or manifestation of
the Divine. The stories or legends that under gird most religious traditions often tell of epiphanies in dramatic, and sometimes literally
earthshaking ways. Moses' encounter with Yahweh in the form of a burning bush, from which Yahweh commands Moses to be the liberator of His
People from bondage, is regarded as the epiphany that in time brought about
the creation of the Jewish faith. For Christians one of the defining epiphanies of their religion comes in the story of an angel appearing to Mary to
announce to her that she is to give birth to the Son of God. Mary's epiphany
is celebrated by Catholic Christians as The Annunciation. When Siddhartha,
meditating beneath a Bodhi tree received his enlightenment, or awakening,
as to what he perceived as being the true nature of existence, this realization
was the epiphany from which Buddhism emerged.

Epiphanies, however, are not reserved for the founders, or progeni-
tors, of major world religions. This is a good thing. And they need not be
accompanied by the dramatic overtures that are often ascribed to them in
the accounts and stories of traditional religions. This, too, is a good thing.
Epiphanies are human realizations. They often occur in a chance encounter,
an unexpected appearance, or even a quick side-glance in which we hear a
finger-snap, or see a light come on, and our world-view, or perspective on

life, is significantly altered. Such epiphanies do not always bring us new insight so much as remind us of truths that we have allowed to remain buried in our minds and souls.

This is an account of a chance encounter that became an epiphany for one Beat writer. In the fall of 1955 three young men, poets and writers in the early stages of their careers, were taking a walk through a dirty, grimy rail yard waterfront area in San Francisco. One of them, Allen Ginsberg, happened to notice a single sunflower, covered with dirt and grime, standing alone. He breaks away from his companions, Jack Kerouac and Philip Whalen, for a closer look. Ginsberg, if the accounts of this encounter are correct, had never seen a sunflower before. He had, however, had a very dramatic and poetic encounter with a sunflower some seven years earlier as he was reading William Blake's poem, *Ah, Sunflower* in a New York City East Harlem apartment in the summer of 1948. Blake's two verse poem reads:

> Ah, Sunflower, weary of time,
> Who countest the steps of the sun,
> Seeking after that sweet golden clime
> Where the traveler's journey is done.
>
> Where the youth pined away with desire,
> And the pale virgin shrouded in snow,
> Arise from these graves and aspire
> Where my Sunflower wishes to go!

According to Ginsberg biographer Barry Miles the experience of reading this poem, which both included and transcended its actual words, affected Ginsberg in a way that recalls Siddhartha's enlightenment. Ginsberg, again according to Miles, saw himself as Blake's sunflower, "weary of time" while also "seeking after that sweet golden clime." As Mr. Ginsberg described the experience: "I suddenly realized that *this* existence was *it*! This was the moment I was born for. This initiation, this consciousness of being alive unto myself. The spirit of the universe was what I was born to realize."

Blake's poetic image of a sunflower blew open Ginsberg's "doors of perception" (to use another Blakean reference) of the very nature and spirit of the universe itself. By flashing on a realization of himself *as* the sunflower,

Ginsberg also realized his connection with, and his being an integral part of, the Web of Life itself. This was the epiphany that served to launch his calling and career as a poet.

Then, seven years later, in the company of two of his closest companions and literary soul-mates, Allen Ginsberg encountered an actual, and very earthly, sunflower. The encounter provided yet another epiphany for him. But this one, even with the same object or image of a sunflower, was of a quite different nature. As Allen would describe it in the poem he wrote several hours later, this encounter with a sunflower takes place as:

> I walked on the banks of the tincan banana dock and sat down
>   under the huge shade of a Southern Pacific locomotive to
>   look at the sunset over the box house hills and cry.
> Jack Kerouac sat beside me on a busted rusty iron pole...
> The oily water on the river mirrored the red sky...
>   no fish in that stream...
> Look at the Sunflower, he [Kerouac] said, there was a dead gray shadow
>   against the sky, big as a man, sitting dry on top of a pile of
>   ancient sawdust—
> I rushed up enchanted—it was my first sunflower, memories
>   of Blake—my visions—Harlem...
>
> and the gray Sunflower poised against the sunset, crackly bleak
>   and dusty with the smut and smog and smoke of olden
>   locomotives in its eye—
> corolla of bleary spikes pushed down and broken like a battered
>   crown, seeds fallen out of its face, soon-to-be-toothless
>   mouth as sunny air, sunrays obliterated on its hairy head
>   like a dried spider web,
> leaves stuck out like arms out of the stem, gestures from the
>   sawdust, broke pieces of plaster fallen out of the black
>   twigs, a dead fly in its ear,
> Unholy battered old thing you were, my sunflower, O my soul,
>   I loved you then!
> The grime was no man's grime but death and human
>   locomotives.

This is one sad and sorry sunflower! It is also a far cry from the poetic, idealized, and romanticized sunflower Allen had encountered via William Blake seven years earlier. Ginsberg comes upon this second sunflower as the first stage of his poetic career is coming into full flower. By the summer of 1954 Allen had relocated from his home base in New York City—after a stay in Mexico, and then a six week visit with the Cassadys in San Jose—to the San Francisco Bay Area. He lived for a time in San Francisco and then moved to a rented cottage in Berkeley. During this time he composed what proved to be some of his most enduring poetic achievements: *Howl for Carl Solomon, America, A Supermarket in California, A Cottage in Berkeley,* and *Sunflower Sutra,* which Ginsberg biographer Michael Schumacher calls "the most remarkable of Ginsberg's Berkeley poems." Although primarily an East Coast guy, Ginsberg became one of the central figures in the San Francisco Poetry Renaissance of the mid-1950s. Kerouac catches this Renaissance as well as he passes through the Bay Area in the fall of 1955. This was when he, Allen, and Phil Whalen took their *Sunflower Sutra* walk.

The title of the poem itself is an indication of the interest in, and attraction to, Buddhism that Ginsberg first experienced at this point in his life, and which remained with him throughout his life. As Buddhist scholar Gary Gach explains it, the term "sutra" derives from the Sanskrit term for thread. On the literal level it means the thread that strings such objects as prayer beads or jewels together. Gach goes on to explain that this root meaning, in Buddhist terminology, is expanded to connote a story, or a tale, or a "yarn" that is strung together, as it were, by a continuing, ongoing theme. By calling his poem *Sunflower Sutra* Ginsberg is using Buddhist language to denote that he is telling a tale in which he first connects with, and then moves on from, his initial Blakean sunflower encounter.

To return, then, to the poem. The first pivotal line, posed as a question, comes after Ginsberg has practically exhausted himself—to say nothing of his readers—describing all of the ugly detritus of civilization that has been heaped upon the initial, naturalistic perfection of the sunflower ("A perfect beauty of a sunflower! a perfect excellent lovely sunflower existence!"):

> Poor dead flower? when did you forget you were a flower? when
> did you look at your skin and decide you were an impotent

dirty old locomotive?

To grasp the essence of this poem I suggest that you close your eyes for a moment or two and repeat several times to yourself Ginsberg's question, "When did you forget you were a flower?" and see where it takes you. When did you forget who or what it was you really felt yourself to be? When did you forget the sensation of being truly alive? When did you forget about your inherent worth, dignity, and holiness? Perhaps Ginsberg himself was sensing the distance between Blake's sunflower and the sunflower he sees here, struggling for its existence in the midst of all that would deny its existence.

As the image of Blake's sunflower accorded Ginsberg an awareness of his union with all of Being—as he maintained it did—perhaps it was this beaten up sunflower, standing forlornly on the "banks of a tincan banana dock," that brought to his awareness all that still stands in the way of that union. "When did you forget you were a flower?" It's a question we can all ask as we seek some accord between our timeless, eternal self and our earth-bound and time-bound self with which we also live. Ginsberg's question is really a challenge for us to remember who and what we ultimately are, and the Universe to which we ultimately belong, even as we live in our "skin of grime."

Ginsberg then moves from his question to announcing a "sermon":

> So I grabbed up the skeleton thick sunflower and stuck it at my
>   side like a scepter,
> and deliver my sermon to my soul, and Jack's soul too, and anyone
>   who'll listen...

This is the sermon he delivers:

> —We are not our skin of grime, we're not our dread bleak dusty
>   imageless locomotive, we're all beautiful golden sunflowers
>   inside, we're blessed by our own seed & golden hairy naked
>   accomplishment bodies....

"We are not our skin of grime." This is the second pivotal line in the poem, and the response to the "When did you forget...?" question. Ginsberg recovers the meaning of his initial, Blakean sunflower in the face of this grime laden, all-too-earthly sunflower. He asserts the primacy of his, and by extension, our "golden hairy naked accomplishment bodies" in the face of all the grime, as it were, that our bodies, and selves, accumulate in the course of living. Grime or no grime, he maintains, "we're all beautiful golden sunflowers inside."

Well, yes we are, and I've needed this reminder, courtesy of Mr. Ginsberg, on many occasions in my life. But I'm not sure that line is the last word, or even the truest word, on who we are as human beings.

This is my favorite Allen Ginsberg poem, not because I completely accept its sentiments, as captivating and enticing as they are, but because I struggle with them and argue with them. The question for Ginsberg, and his readers, is: Does the grime we accumulate, and the scars we come to bear, over the course of our lifetimes make us more or less authentically human? *Sunflower Sutra* implies that the sunflower has lost its essential "sunflower-ness" because it has to live out its existence in a fallen, corrupted-by- civilization, and "un-holy" world—to the point that it has even forgotten that it was/is a sunflower at all. Worldly grime, in other words, robs us of our humanity, or human dignity, and our human holiness to the point that we forget we even possess these things.

But could it also be that the worldly grime that befalls us, and the worldly scars we come to accumulate, are the very things that *give* us our humanity, or that *enhance* our humanity?

As unlikely a pairing as it may seem, I'd like to offer a passage from Shakespeare's *Henry V* as a counterpoint to Ginsberg's *Sunflower Sutra*. The central event in *Henry V* is the Battle of Agincourt, fought on October 25, 1415. It was one of the more significant battles of the Hundred Years War between England and France. On the eve of the battle, which also happens to be the eve of the Feast of St. Crispian, Shakespeare's King Henry, in the course of a rather lengthy soliloquy, says:

> This day is call'd the feast of Crispian.
> He that outlives this day, and comes safe home,
> Will stand tip-toe when this day is named...
> He that shall live this day, and see old age...
> Will yearly on the vigil feast greet his neighbors,
> And say, 'To-morrow is Saint Crispian.'
> Then he will strip his sleeve and show his scars,

And say, 'These wounds I had on Crispian's day.'...
He'll remember, with advantages,
What feats he did that day.

For Shakespeare's King Henry it is the worldly wounds and scars (and grime?) we accumulate that cause us to "remember with advantages" who we once were and still are, rather than forget. Just as no one gets out of this life alive, no one gets out of this life unscathed, unscarred, or free of grime either.

Another of my colleagues in the Unitarian Universalist ministry, the Rev. Clarke Dewey Wells, drew on this Shakespearean passage in a New Year's meditation he composed many years ago, and which is timely as ever:

> We cannot enter the New Year smooth as babes, but we do enter as survivors, often enriched, tougher, wiser, and seasoned by life's struggles, readier for the time to come. Our scars signal more than lamentation; not injury but renewal, not grief but reconciliation, not ruin but restoration, not the old year's accumulation of woe, but the new year's reality of healing, strength, and hope.

Might one see Allen Ginsberg's sunflower as a survivor, seasoned by life's struggles, just as easily, and truthfully, as seeing it as an "unholy old thing"? Could it be a symbol of "healing, strength, and hope" as well as a "broken...battered crown"? Yes, Ginsberg is right to say that we are not our coats of grime. But neither, to use Rev. Wells's imagery, are we "smooth as babes" either. The truth here, as I've come to see it anyway, is that we are not fully defined by either our "beautiful golden hairy naked accomplishment-bodies" or by our coats of grime. Authentic human living takes place in the interplay between the two. One of the many challenges of the human spirit is learning how to meaningfully live in that breach.

All that being said, I continue to be both moved and strengthened by Ginsberg's simple question of "When did you forget you were a flower?" Keeping this question before me, in fact, makes the scars and grime that come my way a means of survival and renewal rather than injury. I refuse to be finally defined by my coat of grime, but neither do I deny it. As romantically attractive, or seductive, the purity of a "perfect sunflower" world may seem at times, I have cast my lot—both for better and for worse—with the realities of twenty-first-century civilization. A coat of grime is the trade-off in such a deal. Yes, I need to feel blessed by my "golden hairy naked accomplishment" body; but I'm shaped and blessed by my scars as well.

So be it.

CHAPTER EIGHT

Death, Life, and Lawrence Ferlinghetti

When the year ends in the number four, and the day is June 6, many of us living in the United States, as well as people in many parts of Western Europe, stop what we're doing at least long enough to remember, and think about, D-Day. June 6, 1944. Under the command of General Dwight Eisenhower—who would later become the thirty-fourth President of the United States—the Allied Forces, largely of American and British composition, crossed the English Channel to invade the German-occupied beaches of France. Following horrific losses of lives on both sides the Allies prevailed, the German hold on France was broken, and the war turned in the Allies favor. Just a little over one year later World War II ended.

As each ten-year span of time goes by the observances of this event—indeed, one of the more momentous events of the twentieth century—seem to keep getting more elaborate, even as, ironically enough, the ranks of the actual soldier survivors of D-Day keep diminishing. The D-Day observances of 1994 and 2004 provided United States Presidents Bill Clinton and George W. Bush each a dramatic moment in the international spotlight; and neither of them had been born at the time of the event itself. I still find myself moved by these observances; not so much by the speeches of politicians but by the pictures and images of the increasingly aging veterans of D-Day as they walk amongst the thousands of grave markers of those killed on that day. I'm sure many of them probably wonder why they were given so many more decades to live, love, work, and raise families, while so many of their young comrades wound up in the ground just beyond the beaches they stormed.

In addition to all this I cannot think of D-Day without also thinking about a 25-year-old Lieutenant Commander in the United States Navy who commanded a submarine chaser during the Normandy invasion. He was from Yonkers, New York. He was an Eagle Scout. He'd already spent some time in college before joining the Navy in order to lend his support to the war effort. He managed to survive the D-Day invasion and safely came home once the war had ended.

Based solely on these tidbits of information one could easily assume that this young Lieutenant Commander, upon arriving back home, would complete his education and find his niche in the ethos of the post-World War II America that was being presided over by his one-time Supreme Allied Commander, General Eisenhower. Perhaps the Lieutenant Commander would return to one of the aforementioned D-Day observances to take his own walk among the graves and do his own musings.

Well, as that rental car commercial once put it, not exactly. Yes, he did continue his college education, with the help of the G.I. Bill, by attending the Sorbonne in Paris after the war. He had spent some of his childhood years in France. And, to be sure, he's done a lot of his own musings; many of which have taken the form of his sometimes whimsical, and sometimes caustically cutting, poems. United States Navy Lieutenant Commander Lawrence Ferlinghetti, the Eagle Scout college boy from Yonkers, New York, became Lawrence Ferlinghetti, first Poet Laureate of San Francisco. He was one of those returning soldiers for whom the trauma of war caused him to question the ethic of war making itself. In Ferlinghetti's case, his poetic sensibilities were awakened, due in part to his wartime experiences.

Ferlinghetti also became the founder and owner of San Francisco's unofficial Beat Headquarters, the City Lights Bookstore, which he and a partner opened in 1953. Being so situated also made him the mid-wife of the West Coast Beat Generation movement.

What happened here to turn a military man into a poet? As defining as the D-Day experience was for many of the soldiers who were a part of it and who survived, Ferlinghetti's defining war moment came over a year later after he'd been relocated to Nagasaki, Japan, shortly after the atomic bomb had been dropped on that city. In a 2001 interview for *The San Francisco*

Reader Lawrence was questioned about that experience by Jeff Troiano. When asked how his short stay at Nagasaki affected him as his life unfolded after the War Ferlinghetti replied:

> Before I was at Nagasaki I was a good American boy. I was an Eagle Scout. I was the commander of a sub chaser in the Normandy invasion. Anyone who saw Nagasaki would suddenly realize that they'd been kept in the dark by the United States government as to what atomic bombs can do.

In an earlier chapter I suggested that part of what gave rise to the Beat movement in America was an awareness of the human capacity to inflict death on a scope and scale that had been previously unimaginable. In some minds this newly acquired capacity to bring about mega-death called into question the very meaning of life itself. From the Holocaust to Hiroshima/ Nagasaki, human life had been made to look more cheap and expendable than it ever had been. But while such thoughts played out in some minds they did not do so in the majority of American minds. The larger cultural response, to which I've also alluded earlier, to this mega-death awareness was an odd combination of denial and paranoia. The denial part was to get back to normal as quickly as possible as though nothing had happened at all; while just below this veneer of denial was the widespread paranoia that The Communists might drop a bomb on us just as we had done to the Japanese people. The way to deal with such paranoia, of course, was to make sure that our democratic, God-fearing, Christian, capitalist atomic bombs were bigger, more powerful, and more destructive than their totalitarian, atheistic, Communist atomic bombs.

So when, in his mid-1950s poem, *America*, Allen Ginsberg declared, "America...go fuck yourself with your atom bomb," it wasn't just his choice of words that was considered obscene. [A quick side observation: Just how obscene can the expression "go fuck yourself" be these days when, in June, 2004, the Vice President of the United States, Dick Cheney, used these very words in the chambers of the United States Senate in addressing Senator Patrick Leahy, and then said he felt better for having said it?] Anyway, in the minds of conventional citizens, Ginsberg's deeper obscenity was his castigation, and his ridiculing, of an entire cultural ethos. But if we play around a bit with the word "obscene" we can get an interesting variation on it. The word *scena* in Latin refers to the scenery on a stage, or in some cases, to the stage itself. The Latin prefix *ab* means, among other things, away from. *Ab-scena*, taken together, means off-stage, or away from the scene. Ginsberg, and the Beats in general, were standing away from, or counter to, the predominant social, politial, cultural, and spiritual scene of the 1950s. They were looking to make their voices heard from the off-stage wings even as the main act was being played out. They were speaking, that is to say, *ab scena*.

In addition to being one of those post-World War II off-stage voices, Lawrence Ferlinghetti also provided, and continues to provide, one of the major channels of expression for those voices through his City Lights Press and Bookstore. Lawrence's reaction to his Nagasaki experience was, and is, in many respects a microcosm of what the Beats expressed as a whole. The Beats looked for ways to affirm life, to find meaning in life, and to keep faith with life, in the face of death on such a scale that it threatened to render life meaningless. Ferlinghetti's mistrust of, and disdain for, political and governmental authority (i.e. being "kept in the dark by the United States government as to what atom bombs can do.") also found expression in some quarters of the wider Beat movement.

I believe Ferlinghetti would shy away from, if not outright disavow, the designation as a spirit guide. Much of his writing, as well as much of what is published by his City Lights Press, have a decidedly more political, than a religious or spiritual, tone. At the same time I feel the most religious act or stance one can take is to affirm the preciousness of life in the face of death; and this stance is the underpinning factor in many of Lawrence's poems and essays.

In fact, Ferlinghetti was an early spirit guide for me before I even realized he played such a role in my life. I first heard the name Ferlinghetti uttered in my sophomore year of college, circa 1964, when an English professor-in-residence, who was spending a year on my campus while on leave from a university in England, read *Christ Climbed Down*. This was one of Lawrence's poems from an early, and still the best known, collection of his work called *A Coney Island of the Mind*. At the time I was still firmly ensconced in the born-again Christian, evangelical Baptist stage of my life (which actually served me quite well for a time).

The image of Jesus Christ climbing down from a Christmas tree struck me as highly sacrilegious. Somehow, I took it as a parody of his hanging on the cross. In my mind at that time, Christ hanging on the cross was not something to be parodied under any circumstances. But, even in my near-fundamentalist mind, I realized there was something I wasn't quite getting in the closing lines that maybe wasn't quite so sacrilegious after all:

> Christ climbed down
> from His bare Tree
> this year
> and softly stole away into
> some anonymous Mary's womb again
> where in the darkest night
> of everybody's anonymous soul
> He awaits again
> an unimaginable
> and impossibly
> Immaculate Reconception
> the very craziest
> of Second Comings.

The idea that the Second Coming of Christ could be the rebirth of the spirit of Jesus Christ in "everybody's anonymous soul," rather than some hugely cosmic event as foretold in the Book of Revelations, proved to be one of the first cracks in my religious consciousness. Some forty years later I'm a humanistically minded Unitarian Universalist minister. Ferlinghetti was among those who first forced open the door of my mind and soul before I even knew who the guy was.

In two basic areas, then, I see Lawrence Ferlinghetti taking on the role of spirit guide. The first I just mentioned, his celebrating a kind of whimsical sacredness of life in the face of death. Recall again my colleague, Rev. Forrest Church's, definition of religion as "our human response to the dual reality of being alive and knowing that we will die." This definition plays itself out in many of Ferlinghetti's poems, and none better than the one from the *Coney Island...* collection beginning with the words, "The world is a beautiful place to be born into..." The poem goes on to juxtapose expressions of that beauty alongside the various deaths-in-life that are also visited upon us in the course of living:

The world is a beautiful place
                              to be born into
        if you don't mind happiness
                              not always being so much fun...

        The world is a beautiful place
                                   to be born into
            if you don't mind some people dying
                                        all the time
                or maybe only starving
                                   some of the time
                which isn't half so bad
                                   if it isn't you.

    Oh the world is a beautiful place
                                   to be born into
            if you don't much mind
                        a few dead minds
                in the higher places
                              or a bomb or two
                now and then
                              in your upturned faces
        or other such improprieties
                              as our Name Brand society
                is prey to
                              with its men of distinction
            and its men of extinction
                              and its priests
            and other patrolmen
                              and its various segregations
        and congressional investigations
                              and other constipations
                that our fool flesh
                              is heir to
    Yes the world is the best place of all

                              for a lot of such things as
          making the fun scene
                         and making the love scene
       and making the sad scene
                     and singing low songs and having inspirations
          and walking around
                    looking at everything
                              and smelling flowers
       and goosing statues
                    and even thinking
                              and kissing people and
          making babies and wearing pants
                              and waving hats and
             dancing
                    and going swimming in rivers
          on picnics
             in the middle of the summer
       and just generally
             'living it up.'
    Yes
       but then right in the middle of it
             comes the smiling

          mortician.

Religion is our human response to the dual reality of being alive and
knowing that we will die. It is how we choose to live, that is to say, in the face
of our mortality. Religion is how we say 'yes' to life in the face of all that would
deny life. For all of the sermons I've constructed around this topic during my
years in the ministry I've yet to find a better expression of this understanding
of religion than in the words of this particular poem of Ferlinghetti's.

Religion is also about transformation, of both the self and society;
a role and task I feel the poet is called to play. Both religion and poetry
reveal the eternal in the temporal and the divine in the mundane, and
Lawrence Ferlinghetti is especially gifted in opening our eyes to this kind
of seeing. Numerous examples could be cited, but this short one from his
Transformations in Paris will suffice:

The white sun of Paris
softens sidewalks
stretches white shadows on skylights
traps a black cat on a distant balcony

And the whole city sleeping drifts
through white space
like a lost dirigible
unconscious of
the immense mystery.

The transformation being offered here is a transformation of consciousness whereby in the sunlight shining through a city one becomes aware of "the immense mystery" in which we each and all live and move and have our being. But it is more than individual transformation, vital as that is, for which the poet strives; it is the transformation of society and the world as well. In his capacity as San Francisco's Poet Laureate, Lawrence wrote an occasional column for the *San Francisco Chronicle*. In the one for December 19, 1999, titled "Can Poetry Really Change the World?" he wrote:

> There are those, including myself, who believe in poets as the antennae of the race, as the conscience of society, or at least as Jack Kerouac said, 'the great rememberer redeeming life from darkness'...Thus we realize how the greatest poets not only change the way we see the world, but also cause us to question our perception and interpretation of everyday reality. And we realize that the greatest poetry subverts the dominant paradigm, ultimately challenges the status quo of the world, and transforms it into something new and strange.

Redeem life from darkness...question our perception and interpretation of everyday reality...subvert the dominant paradigm...(and) challenge the status quo of the world... These are ultimately spiritual challenges and undertakings in that they call for a transformation of consciousness in terms of how we perceive and relate to the world. This is what religion, at its best, does; this is what the spiritual journey is really about—the transformation of consciousness. This is why the best of our poets are also our spirit guides; and I place many of the Beats, Lawrence Ferlinghetti included, in that category.

Carrying forth such a spiritual challenge also proves to be a very worldly and earthly undertaking as well, as Ferlinghetti's life and work well demonstrate. His City Lights Press published Allen Ginsberg's *Howl* within a few months of its first being read at the Six Gallery reading in October of 1955 in San Francisco. Talk about subverting the dominant paradigm! Ginsberg's *Howl*, as has been noted, was really a scream that cut through the aforementioned veneer of denial and paranoia of the 1950s. For such an act of subversion Ferlinghetti and one of his City Lights associates, Shig Muaro, were hit with an obscenity trial in early 1957. They were eventually acquitted. Their acquittal was more than just a legal victory, important as that was. It was also an assurance that those transformative, off-stage, voices would continue to be heard. Ferlinghetti's willingness to take the risks involved in publishing this work was a truly prophetic act.

Nearly a half-century later Ferlinghetti remains hard at his work of transformation and subversion of the dominant paradigm. The current dominant paradigm is the War on Terror, which is the heir to the 1950s War on Communism. Like Communists in the 1950s who wanted to do bad things to America, today terrorists also wish to do bad things to us—as they indeed have. But just as anti-communism harmed America and the spirit of American liberty in the 1950s and 60s more than communism itself, so has our current War on Terror become a war on ourselves. And Lawrence Ferlinghetti is still there in 2005 preaching the word. At the initiation of our war against Iraq he penned the poem *Dragon's Teeth*. In view of the Iraqi insurgency that has been ongoing since we invaded that country his words could not have been more prophetic.

A headless man is running
down the street
He is carrying his head
in his hands
A woman runs after him
She has his heart
in her hands
The bombs keep falling
sowing hate
And they keep running

down the streets
Not the same two people
but thousands of others & brothers
All running
from the bombs that keep falling
sowing pure hate

And for every bomb that's dropped
up spring a thousand Bin Ladens
a thousand new terrorists
Like dragon's teeth spring up
From which armed warriors spring up
Crying for blood

As the smart bombs sowing hate
Keep falling and falling and falling.

Similar sentiments are expressed in *Speak Out!*:

And a vast paranoia sweeps across the land
And America turns the attack on its Twin Towers
Into the beginning of the Third World War
The war with the Third World...

And the terrorists in Washington
Are shipping out the young men
To the killing fields again

And no one speaks

And they are rousting out
All the ones with turbans
And they are flushing out
All the strange immigrants

And they are shipping all the young men
To the killing fields again

And no one speaks

And when they come to round up
All the great writers and poets and painters
The National Endowment of the Arts of Complacency
Will not speak

While all the young men
Will be killing all the young men
In the killing fields again

So now is the time for you to speak
All you lovers of liberty
All you lovers of the pursuit of happiness
All you lovers and sleepers
Deep in your private dream
Now is the time for you to speak.
O silent majority
Before they come for you!

I have to wonder if these times are discouraging ones for Ferlinghetti. A man who risked his life for his country in the Second World War has now twice seen the liberties, for which he ostensibly fought, undermined by fear mongering in the highest of places. Those "few dead minds in the higher places or a bomb or two now and then in your upturned faces" are, tragically, still very much with us. In his *San Francisco Reader* interview with Jeff Troiano he was asked: "Is the current threat to our civil liberties comparable to what you experienced in the early '50s?" His reply was sobering: "No, it's much worse. That was nothing back then. President Eisenhower's reign was very stultifying; there was lots of unspoken censorship. But today Eisenhower looks like an angel compared to these bandits who are now running Washington."

As I've already suggested, one of the roles and tasks of a spirit guide is to continue to hold up a vision of what Jesus called "the abundant life" even in the face of some of the more cruel and senseless forms of death. Lawrence's poetic playfulness still needs to stay in play—now more than ever. In the face of all that would deny the graciousness and goodness of life, perhaps the most radical and spiritually transforming act one can perform is to keep that playfulness, that gracious, and that goodness still in our conscious awareness—just so we'll know what it is we're still standing for and fighting for.

I am waiting for my case to come up
and I am waiting
for a rebirth of wonder
and I am waiting for someone
to really discover America...

and I am waiting
for them to prove
that God is really American...

I am waiting
for the meek to be blessed and inherit the earth
without taxes
and I am waiting for forests and animals
to reclaim the earth as theirs
and I am waiting for a way to be devised
to destroy all nationalisms
without killing anybody
and I am waiting
for linnets and planets to fall like rain
and I am waiting for lovers and weepers
to lie down together again
in a new rebirth of wonder...

and I am waiting
for Aphrodite
to grow live arms
at a final disarmament conference
in a new rebirth of wonder

I am waiting
to get some intimations

of immortality
by recollecting my early childhood
and I am waiting
for the green mornings to come again
youth's dumb green fields come back again...
and I am waiting for the last long careless rapture
and I am perpetually waiting
for the fleeing lovers on the Grecian Urn
to catch up to each other at last
and embrace
and I am awaiting
perpetually and forever
a renaissance of wonder.

These words were published in 1958. It is all still worth waiting for, and worth struggling after.

CHAPTER NINE

Neal Cassady and the Mystical Madness of the Moment

"**H**ave you ever seen anyone like Cody Pomeray?... Oh life, who is that?" So wrote Jack Kerouac in his great work and tribute to his soul-mate companion of the road Neal Cassady, as Cody Pomeray, in *Visions of Cody*. Countless individuals have been trying to answer Kerouac's questions ever since. In fact, the questions are tougher now than when Kerouac first set them forth. There has been such an extensive mythology built up around the figure of Neal Cassady—whose burnt-at-both-ends candle was extinguished just four days short of his 42nd birthday in 1968—that the last word on who he was will most likely never ever be written or spoken.

In this one respect at least Cassady's story can be likened to that of another holy man, Jesus of Nazareth. Most of what is known about Jesus is filtered through the mythology that came to surround his life story in the decades following his death, to the point that the actual truth of his earthly life will, like Cassady's, never be fully known. Despite, or because, of this—and it is some of both—a religion eventually came to be established in Jesus' name. While there is not, to the best of my knowledge, a "Church of Neal Cassady" (which is not to say it couldn't happen), Neal's life has become so intertwined with legend that is it difficult to sort out who he was from what legend has made of him in the nearly four decades since his death. But then, we all achieve our immortality in the stories that are told about us once our earthly time has passed, however reality based or not those stories may be. Neal Cassady is no different in this regard; it's just that his stories have attained a certain mythic quality, elevating him to the realm of spirit guide.

Since I did not discover the Beats until just after Neal's death, I never knew the man. But the reactions I get in speaking with men and women who knew him fascinate me. There's often a smile, a rather wistful look in their eyes as they stare upwards, a few shakes of the head, and then a reaching for words that seem just beyond the grasp of the mind. These are some of the same gestures and body language I've observed in persons who are trying to describe a profoundly religious experience they've had without quite being able to articulate it. In his outstanding history of The Grateful Dead, *A Long Strange Trip*, author Dennis McNally notes, "Neal Cassady was very possibly the most highly evolved personality they (The Dead) would ever meet, and was certainly among their most profound life influences other than the psychedelic experience itself."

But when it comes to some of the students I've had in my Beat Literature classes over the years, I get quite a different reaction on occasion, especially from the women. They generally say something like: how could Kerouac, through the character of *On the Road's* Dean Moriarty, glorify, if not worship, such psychopathic behavior as demonstrated by Moriarty's prototype, Neal Cassady? Here's a guy who, on a whim, loots the family savings account to buy a brand new car in San Francisco and then goes on a cross-country tear leaving his wife and infant daughter high and dry and broke. And who, on yet another of those meaingless continental meanderings, supposedly marries another woman in New York—with whom he's fathered a child—after obtaining what proved to be an invalid Mexican divorce from his wife in San Francisco. He then immediately returns to his San Francisco wife! This is supposed to make him a candidate for sainthood?!

More than one of the women in my classes have cheered on the *On the Road* character Galatea Dunkel (Helen Hinkle) in the passage where, completely fed up with the guy who she feels has corrupted and used her husband Ed (Al Hinkle), lets Dean/Neal have it with both barrels:

> You have absolutely no regard for anybody but yourself and your
> damned kicks. All you think about is what's hanging between your legs

and how much money or fun you can get out of people and then you just throw them aside...It never occurs to you that life is serious and there are some people trying to make something decent of it instead of just goofing all the time.

Galatea/Helen is indeed being a truth teller here. She makes accusations that any reasonably minded, decent living person would make after witnessing some of Neal's antics. Neal/Dean, in this passage, has nothing to say in his defense back to Helen; and Jack, while knowing that there is far more to Neal than what Helen is speaking to, opts for silence himself. It is only in his mind that Jack plays off of Helen's comment about Neal "just goofing all the time" and labels Neal as "The Holy Goof." The operative word there, of course, is Holy. But more on this later.

Mrs. Hinkle's truth, on target as it may have been at the moment she was speaking it, is not the whole truth, however. There was yet another part of Neal Cassady that did try hard to "make something decent" of his life in accordance with the conventional standards of decency of his time. He married a woman, Carolyn Robinson Cassady, who had come from a very refined, well-educated background, and who had a Masters Degree in Fine Arts and Theater Arts from the University of Denver. They had three children for whom he attempted, with a measure of success, to be a loving, supportive and even protective father. Among the many and varied figures associated with the Beat Generation, the thing to note about Neal Cassady is that, for a certain stretch of his life, he got up in the morning, got dressed for work, and went off to earn a paycheck that paid the mortgage on a ranch house in Los Gatos, California and bought the groceries for his wife and kids. You can't get much more "un-Beat" than that. Neal was, in other words, no Maynard G. Krebs with an adolescent aversion to work.

Cassady's son, John Allen, remembers his father home-schooling, so to speak, his children in their religious education. Neal was raised Catholic, and had even been an altar boy in his growing up days in Denver. And while his own religious journey moved well beyond his upbringing, he wanted his son and his two daughters to have some kind of foundation, which he and Carolyn attempted to provide. As John Allen tells it:

> He (Neal) would sit us on the couch and pace around talking (Edgar)

Cayce, the Dead Sea Scrolls, reincarnation, and the like. It was church for
an hour and he was our Sunday School teacher. We had to sit there for an
hour and I'm wanting to go out and see my gang friends at the tree house.
But I had to get my religious instruction first.

This story, in fact, demonstrates as well as any how much Neal aspired
to be the provider for a respectable home and family. As Carolyn Cassady
recalls in some personal correspondence, "I realized later in our lives that
from his childhood, one of the driving motivations of Neal's life was to become 'respectable.' Hence his early fascination with books, his polishing his
speech, etc. It explains, also, why he was attracted to me." So, Neal was a
home owner, a family man, and a man with a perfect ten year employment
record on the Southern Pacific Railroad.

Neal and Carolyn discovered the works of Edgar Cayce in 1954 by way
of the book *Many Mansions* by Gina Cerminara. This discovery proved to
be the beginning of a wide ranging religious exploration by the Cassadys that
included the writings of Cayce, while also going well beyond them. In time
it came to encompass the lore of occult teachers whose writings had been
in print for centuries. It was this religious dimension that Neal and Carolyn,
in turn, sought to pass on to their children—just as any loving and caring
parents would. While Carolyn does not ignore the various other aspects
of Neal's life, the home-and-family side of Neal is well demonstrated and
documented in her previously mentioned book *Off the Road—My Years with
Cassady, Kerouac, and Ginsberg* (Penguin Books, 1990).

Helen and Al Hinkle's daughter, Dawn, recalls her times of being at the
Cassady household in Los Gatos, playing with Neal and Carolyn's daughters
Cathleen (Nickname, Cathy) and Jami. She remembers Neal as a humorous
kind of guy, who was fun to be around, and who cared a great deal about his
wife and family. Her feeling is that if Neal hadn't been sent to jail for a couple
of years (1958-60) on a marijuana bust, the family life dimension of his life
would have simply continued on as the kids grew up.

The more one ponders Kerouac's question, "Cody Pomeray ...who is
that?" the more complex, if not indecipherable, it becomes. But I will attempt
at least a thumb-nail sketch of his life here. Neal Cassady literally grew up on
the streets of Denver, Colorado, alternating between the flop houses where

his alcoholic father, a barber, Neal Cassady, Sr., would stay; and at the homes where his mother, sister, and half-siblings lived. His exposure to Catholicism was in part through the Catholic social service agencies that provided various types of care for him during his childhood. As Neal moved into adolescence his base of operation came to be an establishment called Pederson's Pool Hall, where his closest friends were Jim Holmes and Al Hinkle.

Legend, at least, has it that Neal had his first full heterosexual experience at age nine. Less legendary is the fact that by the age of 18 he'd been in and out of various jails and reform schools for stealing hundreds of cars, mostly so he could drive them around Denver and environs for a few hours or days. In addition to his voracious sexual appetite he also discovered, while in reform school, another strong appetite for learning, which he'd had from a very young age, especially in the areas of literature, philosophy, and religion. At a later point in his life, making use of his photographic memory, he could recite all the names of the Popes from Saint Peter to the present.

A Denver high school teacher, Justin Brierley, attempted to nurture Neal's passion for thought and learning, and it was through Brierley that Neal met a Columbia University bound Denver high school student named Hal Chase. Hal Chase is the fourth person in the famous Birth of the Beat Generation photo of Kerouac, Ginsberg, Burroughs, (and Chase), taken near Columbia University in 1944. In 1946, at age 20, Cassady married 16 year old LuAnne Henderson and the two of them later set off from Denver to New York to meet up with Hal Chase. Through Chase Neal came into the orbit of what would later be termed the Beat Generation, and those whom Kerouac, in *On the Road*, called "the mad ones." This meeting up in New York of Kerouac and Cassady led to the cross-country exploits later chronicled in *On the Road*.

From Denver, Neal re-located to San Francisco, following Carolyn Robinson who had also moved there. After being granted an annulment of his marriage to LuAnne, he and Carolyn married and began their family. Through Al Hinkle's connections Neal got a job working on the Southern Pacific railroad. The Cassadys moved to San Jose in 1952 and then settled in Los Gatos the following year. Neal essentially moved between two (at the very least) worlds during the mid 1950s. There was the world of his wife, family, and railroad job. This world took him from the Southern Pacific station in San Jose (about 10 miles from Los Gatos) up to San Francisco on passenger runs. On freight train runs he went as far south as Watsonville and occasionally to San Luis Obispo. Then, there was his free-wheeling, and often sexual philandering world, that was centered in and around the Bay Area. One of the main "other women" in his life during this period was Natalie Jackson, whose tragic suicide (or was it an accidental fall?) in San Francisco is recounted in Kerouac's *The Dharma Bums*.

In September, 1957, Neal Cassady was introduced to the world as Holy Goof "Dean Moriarty" with the publication of *On the Road*. Reflecting both his internal and external split, part of Cassady tried to live down the Dean image while another part of him tried to live up to it.

In April of 1958 Neal was sentenced to a prison term on marijuana related charges. It had started several months earlier when Neal was given $40.00 by a couple of agents to purchase some marijuana for them. Suspecting they were indeed agents, Neal took the money and bet it at a race track instead. Then, in February of '58 he was given a ride from a party in San Francisco by a couple of men to the Southern Pacific depot where he reported for work. In exchange for the ride he gave them a couple of marijuana joints. As he later related to Carolyn, "Then, on the way home it hit me. Something told me they were narcs." The upshot of the whole matter was his eventual arrest for both possession and dealing.

The evidence against him was skimpy at best, but the presiding judge in the case, as Carolyn Cassady reports in her account of the trial, stated that he didn't like Neal's attitude and handed him a five year jail sentence. The actual length of the sentence turned out to be two years, the bulk of which was served at the San Quentin penitentiary on the northern end of San Francisco Bay. The conviction and sentence cost Cassady his job on the Southern Pacific Railroad. It also brought severe economic hardship to his wife and three children for the two years that he ended up doing time until his release in the summer of 1960.

Neal Cassady and Jack Kerouac had just one more extended encounter after Neal's San Quentin stretch. It was in Los Gatos and at Big Sur's Bixby Canyon in the late summer of 1960, and is chronicled in Kerouac's novel *Big Sur* and in Carolyn's *Off the Road*. Jack and Neal would have two more very brief meetings in New York in later years.

But, as of the mid-1960s, the locus of Cassady's life shifted to the doings of the Merry Prankster assemblage that had coalesced around the novelist Ken Kesey in La Honda, California; and the mid-1960s music/rock scene in San Francisco, as primarily epitomized by Jerry Garcia and The Grateful Dead. Neal was the driver for the Merry Prankster's bus, both on its trips in and around the Bay Area as well as its famous cross-country tour in 1964. He became a regular fixture at Dead concerts. Timothy Leary also became a part of Neal's circle of acquaintances at this time. Neal and Carolyn Cassady divorced in 1964. One of his primary women during this stage of Neal's life was Anne Murphy, whom he'd met shortly after his release from jail.

In the latter part of the 1960s the lives of both Neal Cassady and Jack Kerouac began to flame out. For Kerouac it was reclusive alcoholism that finally brought on his demise. For Cassady it was perpetual motion and a variety of drugs that, in time, pointed him down his last path. In a way Neal became a caricature of himself. Part of him seemed to feel he somehow had to live up to the myth of Neal Cassady that was already forming in his lifetime. But there was another part of Neal that simply wanted peace of mind and peace of spirit. He found this, for a time, by way of the explorations he and Carolyn made into spiritual studies that included reading the works of Edgar Cayce and seeking the counsel of Hugh Lynn Cayce. But, tragically, in the end such peace eluded Neal.

In late January of 1968 Neal left the home in Los Gatos, where Carolyn still allowed him to stay on occasion, to go to Mexico. Carolyn recounts that she urged him to make this move to avoid a possible jail sentence due to the various traffic violations he'd accumulated in the years after his release from prison. On his way to Mexico Neal stopped in Los Angeles, where John Bryant had offered him a job helping to distribute an underground newspaper he produced and edited there called *Open City*. One of Bryant's writers was the Los Angeles based poet and novelist Charles Bukowski, one the last persons to see Cassady alive.

Neal's stay in Los Angeles was brief. He headed on to San Miguel de Allende, Mexico. On February 4, 1968, Neal Cassady collapsed and died alongside a stretch of railroad tracks. The actual cause of his death has never been determined. He'd been walking back from a wedding party he'd attended to retrieve some of his belongings from a train station in a nearby village.

In some ways it is easy to see how such a life can become mythologized, if not deified. In one sense Neal's life represents the embodiment of a not uncommon human fantasy—especially (but not exclusively) on the part of males—of a free floating, unconstrained kind of existence. Cassady behind the wheel of a car with an endless road before him, or Cassady in the throes of sexual ecstasy with his most recently seduced woman, clearly plays into such a fantasy. This part of Neal, in fact, initially attracted him to the shy and repressed Jack Kerouac. Neal was one of the mad ones behind whom Jack, by his own account, came "shambling after."

But, as Kerouac would come to see himself, to reduce Neal Cassady to one's projected fantasies (or horrors) about him is to miss the greater essence of the man, and what his life was truly about. As I said at the beginning of this chapter, the question Kerouac asks about Neal/Cody, "Who is that?," will never be fully answered; but I'll put forth my partial attempt.

While Cassady studied Buddhism he never embraced any form of it as a way of life, as Kerouac did for a time. But in his own way Neal attempted to reach the Buddhist ideal of being fully present in the moment with no awareness of, or attention being paid to, either the past or the future. Within Buddhism, and through its varied expressions, this ideal state is pursued through meditation, and disciplined meditative practices so that any awareness of time is placed beyond the machinations of the mind. One method is to cease all motion, both physical and mental; to be perfectly still and aware only of the intake and outflow of one's breathing. Finding the means to do this does move one into a timeless state—if only, ironically enough, for a certain period of time. No one, of course, ever fully escapes his/her time-bound existence except by death; and whatever may or may not lie beyond the cessation of one's earthly life is a matter of personal faith and belief.

Neal Cassady, however, stood the Buddhist ideal of transcending an awareness of time via meditation on its head. For Cassady continuous motion was his means of transcending time, or of stepping outside the workings of time. The direction or purpose of the motion was, at best, a secondary consideration. The image of Neal Cassady at the wheel of the Merry Pranksters' bus with the sole destination of "Further" painted on the front of it captures the point quite well.

One of the crazier episodes in Kerouac's *On the Road* also addresses this matter. After a frantic cross-country ride from San Francisco—in a 1949 Hudson purchased on a whim by cleaning out, as already alluded to, his and Carolyn's savings account—Neal, Al Hinkle, LuAnne Henderson (retrieved in Denver), and Kerouac (picked up in North Carolina) wind up in New York at the end of December, 1948. Allen Ginsberg, as Carlo Marx, confronts Neal/Dean in a mother-hen type of manner demanding to know the "meaning" of such a seemingly meaningless trip. Neal/Dean's response: "No answer—giggles." Jack himself knew that "The madness would lead nowhere." But for Neal the madness of the moment doesn't need to *lead* anywhere. The madness of the moment yields timelessness, and that was the state Neal was reaching for.

Neal/Dean tries to articulate this meaning of madness in a madcap conversation he and Jack have as they bat down the road on their way out of New York: "Everything is fine. God exists. We know time... The thing is not to get hung-up... As we roll along this way I am positive beyond doubt that everything will be taken care of for us... We know America; we're at home..." Jack gets it, but can't completely buy it:

> There was nothing clear about the things he said, but what he meant to say was somehow pure and clear...I had never dreamed Dean would become a mystic. These were the first days of his mysticism, which would lead to the strange, ragged W.C. Fields saintliness of his later days.

Kerouac, in other words, cannot fully embrace Cassady's mystical madness of the moment, but he can still recognize it and see a certain kind of holiness about it.

Talk, for Neal Cassady, was yet another way of transcending time through motion. Another memory John Allen has of his father is from the mid-sixties. Teenage John walked down a street in Santa Cruz, California on his way to do a little surfing, and saw a huge crowd of people gathered in front of an establishment called the Hip Pocket Bookstore. The object of the crowd's attention was John's father, Neal, holding forth on what had come to be known as a Neal Cassady Rap. Cassady would pick up on a thread of thought, a piece of conversation, a fragment of philosophy, etc. and then just go with it in a stream of consciousness flow that James Joyce would quite likely envy. And Neal could apparently also keep the stream going, and somehow keep it linked even as he leapt from one idea to another, in such a way that would be mesmerizing to his listeners.

Here again is a counterpoint to the Buddhist meditation technique of freeing the mind of all thought in order to fully enter the present moment, free of past or future. For Neal, instead of emptying the mind, he gave his mind—and, when he had an audience, his voice—complete free rein to go where it would at the demands, or at the call, of the present moment; not unlike the way he operated a car. Another part of the Cassady lore in this vein is that he could keep several unrelated conversations going at once in a room full of people, much in the same way that a chess master can move around a room from one chessboard to another playing a different game of chess with each of the persons at each of the boards and usually staying ahead in each game. (Cassady was also an accomplished chess player). Having these multitiered conversations was Neal's way of moving in the moment, and fulfilling the moment, without being confined to the moment itself. It was yet another way of his taking the moment outside of time.

Then there was sex. To write of Neal Cassady without mentioning sex would be like writing of Timothy Leary without mentioning LSD. As Kerouac said of Neal in the opening paragraphs of *On the Road*: "To him (Neal/Dean) sex was the one and only holy and important thing in life, although he had to sweat and curse and make a living and so on."

I do not pretend to fully understand the motivation behind Cassady's apparently incessant pursuits of sexual gratification. Some of us, of course, are born with higher sex drives than others; and Neal's, by all indication, was way on the upper end of that scale. In addition, Neal's introduction to his own sexuality was not exactly a healthy one, as partially demonstrated in William Plummer's *The Holy Goof* (Paragon House, 1990). And while concrete evidence for this is hard to come by, there are also reports that at a very young—clearly prepubescent—age he was performing, for nickels and dimes, oral sex for some of the denizens of the Denver flophouses where he lived, off and on, with his father. Taken altogether this does offer one way of looking at Neal Cassady's sexual behavior.

The phrase "childhood sexual abuse" had most likely not been coined in that day, and I seriously doubt that Neal ever regarded himself as an adult survivor (as the current recovery language terms it) of early age sex abuse.

But consider this: survivors of childhood sexual abuse have often been known to act out in one of two very different modes of sexual behavior. One is the eschewing of all things sexual, to the point of not wanting to be touched at all. The other is often overt promiscuity or excessive sexual acting out in their later years; and/or wanting to be sexually available to a wide variety of sexual partners under a variety of circumstances. Cassady's sexual behavior clearly fell in the latter category. He was compulsively heterosexual, for example, but also granted homosexual favors to Allen Ginsberg shortly after the two met. He wanted, that is, to please. He clearly wanted his own pleasure as well. I'm not a therapist, and possess no real in depth or academic knowledge about the effects of childhood sexual abuse or mistreatment; but I have to wonder if, in Neal's case, his myriad pursuits of sexual gratification were attempts to obliterate what may have been painful memories of some of his earliest sexual experiences.

Given all that, I still do not believe that the nature of Neal Cassady's sexuality can be reduced to any one cause or factor. I tend to see his sexual activity as part of that same larger phenomenon that also included his driving, his conversing, and his thought processes—yet another way of Neal responding solely to the call of the moment.

Neal Cassady's life is not one I could emulate. I'm not even sure how long I would have lasted just trying to hang out with him, for that matter. Realities being what they are, I'll never know for sure. We need not be, however, completely simpatico with those whom we look upon as spirit guides. In Cassady's life, or in what I've come to know of it, there are two overlapping phenomena that inform my own spiritual life and journey. In this man's life and way of being we see both the divine and the demonic, as well as the glorious and the desperate, dimensions of living in the Now. Neal knew what it meant to be fully present in the moment, and fully responsive to the call of the moment. And he was as cursed by this characteristic at least as much as he was blessed by it, if not more. Furthermore, he was willing to take his chances with both outcomes. Neal was the one who was willing to step outside of time, and in so doing he showed the rest of us how being in such a place can ennoble us, even as it holds the potential for destroying us.

On of the most poignant passages in all of American literature is Kerouac's description of Dean/Neal standing on a cold New York City street corner in the closing chapter of *On the Road*. He has made another mad-cap cross-country scramble to be with Sal/Jack. But now Sal Paradise has a woman in his life and is trying to settle in for a stretch. He and his woman and another couple are heading off in a limo to a Duke Ellington concert. Dean/Neal fades into the background—alone. The tight-assed moralistic response to Neal/Dean's plight is to say: "It serves the goddamned irresponsible fool right." On one level anyway I guess it does. Neal/Dean's living by impulse does hit a dead end in this instance, leaving him stranded in the cold with nowhere to go. But still, somewhere in the hearts and souls of those in the limo, is at least the intimation that Dean, as desperate and pathetic as his immediate plight is, has tapped into to a level of living that they will never quite know for themselves. It is this gut-level intimation, a few lines later, that has the book end with Sal "think(ing) of Dean Moriarty."

Kerouac's portrayal of Neal in this book has more insight, and subtleties, that he (Kerouac) is generally given credit for showing. Neal/Dean is a heroic figure in that he attempts to live a life beyond the time bound compromises most of us make with life. But he's also a sad and tragic figure in that this very same uncompromising stance ultimately leaves him abandoned. It is an abandonment that Neal has to live with, whether it is in the winter cold of a New York street corner, or in being cold dead beside a Mexican railroad track.

Neal Cassady was either unable and/or unwilling to cut the deal most of us come to in the course of living. He really did try to live out the deal at various times in his life, particularly with his family in Los Gatos. But ultimately the deal eluded him. In Freudian language this is the deal between our Id and our Superego. The impulses of the Id call us to the immediacy and the demands of the moment; to the demands of the Now, that is to say. The Superego orders us to temper those demands: No, not now, that's too impractical, or too irresponsible, or too thoughtless, or too whatever. To paraphrase Henry David Thoreau's well known words, the mass of humanity lives quiet lives of deferred gratification. So when we encounter someone who tries to live, or has to live, somewhere past, or beyond, that delayed gratification deal or cultural compromise, our reactions can range from awe and wonder on the one hand, to disgust and anger on the other. In living the life that he did Neal Cassady made himself the target for both sets of reactions. He died for our fantasies as well as for our self-righteousness. We yearn to be like him and righteously thank God we're not like him all in the same thought or sensation.

The novelist Robert Stone, who briefly knew Cassady during Neal's Prankster phase, refers to Neal as having had a "career as a character in other people's work." This is true, just as it is true that Neal's first published work did not appear until three years after his death with the publication of his partial autobiography, *The First Third*. But, as later publications of Neal Cassady's work have demonstrated, he was truly a man of letters. His volume of correspondence, as shown in his prison letters to Carolyn in *Grace Beats Karma* (Blast Books, 1993) demonstrate he was a truly gifted writer. The publication in 2004 of his *Collected Letters 1944-1967* (Penguin Books) bears this out even further. While many of these letters are to Carolyn, there are dozens also written to Jack Kerouac and Allen Ginsberg. Another set of Neal's letters, *As Ever* (Creative Arts. Berkeley, CA), documents some of his correspondence with Allen Ginsberg. The influence of Cassady's writing on the works of Kerouac and Ginsberg can be clearly seen; and Neal served as an inspiration for numerous other writers as well.

For this, Neal Cassady also paid a price. To return to Stone's observation:

> Kerouac had used him (Cassady), as would Kesey, Tom Wolfe, and I. The persistent calling forth and reinventing his existence was an exhausting process even for such an extraordinary mortal as Neal. Maybe it has earned him the immortality he yearned for. It certainly seems to have shortened his life.

John Bryant learned of Neal's death shortly after Neal departed from his home in Los Angeles, and went on to Mexico. In the next issue of *Open City*, Mr. Bryant offered his own remembrance of Neal, which included the following: "Neal came to a time in his life when he had to face up to the fact that even Dean Moriarty must get older, must adapt to his internal changes...his death on February 4 was, in essence, a refusal to accept that changed condition." True enough, I guess; and one can see Cassady's final refusal as either noble or tragic, heroic or foolhardy. It's certainly a moot point with him at this point. I see it as his last and ultimately—ironically, perhaps—successful attempt to be beyond time and completely in the Now.

As for the rest of us, who continue to keep trying to come up with ways of living betwixt and between our fantasies and our righteousness, perhaps Neal Cassady is somewhere giving us a beatific smile and saying: You're making your choices just as I made mine; and we'll all be on the same side of time in due time.

CHAPTER TEN

Beat Women: Joining the Dance

In 1962 a young woman of 26 saw the publication of her first novel, *Come and Join the Dance*. She had been working on it for a number of years, including the period of time when she'd had a romantic fling with Jack Kerouac just prior to, and in the aftermath of, the publication of *On the Road*. Several years later she would publish another book recounting that period of her life with the title, *Minor Characters*.

This title was Joyce Johnson's tongue-in-cheek characterization of the place and role of women in the overall Beat movement. With some notable exceptions, like Diane di Prima or Denise Levertov, most of the women who are identified as part of the Beat Generation (however much in agreement, or not, they may have been with such a designation) are primarily done so through their relationship with a man—or men—who were a part of that movement. They were, as Joyce Glassman Johnson not so subtly implied, minor characters.

Such women, by and large, did not choose this role for themselves. They were generally relegated to it by the Beat men. Even the most counter of counter-cultural movements still retains some of the blind spots of the culture against which it is ostensibly rebelling or resisting. In the 1950s, and into the early 60s, the assumed primary role of women in mainstream America was that of helpmate and support system for the men, who were unquestionably in charge. For all of their avant-garde strivings, many of the Beats were unable to get past this mainstream cultural assumption themselves.

In more recent years, beginning in the early 1990s, there has been a resurgence of interest in, and attention paid to, the women writers and artists of the Beat era, with some of their writings finally seeing the light of day for the first time. Indeed, some of the more serious scholarly work, commentary, and investigations into the Beat era itself are now being done by women academicians and scholars, as they bring a long neglected feminist perspective to that period of time. For example, I was recently invited to join an organization called The Beat Studies Association. The President, Vice-President, Secretary-Treasurer, and Editor are all women educators.

Acknowledging, then, my deep admiration and appreciation for such scholarly work, it is not my primary intention in this chapter to provide a review, or overview, of it. For those who wish to focus specifically on the role and contributions of women in the Beat movement I recommend, as a good starting point, the book *Women of the Beat Generation,* edited by Brenda Knight with a Foreword by Anne Waldman (Conari Press, 1996). The overarching purpose of this book is to point to some of the spiritual struggles, triumphs, and failures of the Beat Generation writers, male and female, and the continuing importance of their spiritual journeys for those of us on our spiritual paths today.

Of all the chapters I've undertaken I must acknowledge that this is the one I feel the least equipped to write. I cannot experience for myself a woman's consciousness. I think I'd feel the same way if, as a white male, I were attempting to get inside some aspect of the African-American experience in America. At the same time, I find a real kind of courage and power in the works of some of the woman of the Beat era even if I cannot enter into the gender experience that markedly contributed to the production of these works. With an awareness of this limitation, I proceed.

I respect Joyce Glassman Johnson's repeated contention that she does not consider herself to be a Beat writer. But I find in her book, *Come and Join the Dance,* (which was published with her birth name of Joyce Glassman as she had not become Joyce Johnson at that time) a Beat work on par with the late John Clellon Holmes' *Go,* which was published twelve years prior to Ms. Glassman's novel. *Go* is generally regarded as America's first Beat Generation novel.

Ms. Glassman, as noted, worked on her book at the time that she was in a relationship, and having some correspondence, with Jack Kerouac in 1957-58. Their correspondence from those years was published in 2002 under the title *Door Wide Open* (Viking Press, 2002). In their letters Jack offers Joyce encouragement as she writes her novel. By the time it came out several years later, however, their relationship was long gone. While *Come and Join the Dance* never achieved the fame and popularity of *On the Road*, or *Go*, (it had a very limited print run and has long been out of print), it brings a woman's voice, and spirit, to some of the same struggles of the spirit addressed by many of the male Beat writers. The fact that this well written first novel remains out of print indicates to me that the contributions of women to the Beat genre of writing and creativity are yet to be fully realized and appreciated. Admittedly, in *Come and Join the Dance* the terms Beat and Beat Generation are never used or in any way alluded to, but with apologies (if necessary) to Joyce Glassman Johnson I'm treating it as a Beat novel.

To turn, then, to a synopsis the book: Susan Levitt of Cedarhurst, Long Island, New York is about to graduate from an upscale women's college on the upper West Side of Manhattan. While the school is not named in the book its prototype is clearly Barnard College, which Ms. Johnson herself attended in the early 1950s. The Susan Levitt character is in large part a self-portrait of Glassman, drawn from her Barnard days. Susan's counter-point character is a woman named Kay, primarily drawn from the person of a young woman named Elise Cowen, who came from a wealthy, and well-established, Long Island family. Elise and Joyce were close friends for a number of years.

As for the fictitious Miss Levitt, her proud, if somewhat rigid, parents are coming into New York to see their daughter graduate. Before they arrive, however, Susan has to take her final exams, get moved out of her dorm, go to graduation practice, and pack for a solo trip to Paris she's planned as something of a getting-out-of-school celebration, or reward, for herself. But very little of any of it seems real to her. It's all so unreal, in fact, that she walks out of her English final without answering the final essay question. She then proceeds to wander up Broadway with these thoughts in mind:

> What if you lived your entire life completely without urgency? You went to classes, you ate your meals, on Saturday nights a boy you didn't love took you to the movies; and now and then you actually had a con-

versation with somebody. The rest of the time—the hours that weren't accounted for—you spent waiting for something to happen to you; when you were particularly desperate you went out looking for it...

These few lines characterize Susan Levitt's predicament. By extension they portray the predicament of any number of young women, who possessed even a modicum of worldly awareness, and who were coming of age in America during the 1950s. These women knew at some level of their being that they could not adapt to the woman's script the culture of that time had written for them, but they had no other scripts available. Not only were there no scripts, there wasn't even a sufficient language available by which they could express their sensibilities. So, a woman waited for something to happen; or desperately went searching for "it," without even being able to adequately articulate what the "something" or the "it" was. Of course the most likely something to happen to a woman of this era, and societal setting, was to marry a man who was finding his own niche in post-World War II corporate America, and live in a community like Cedarhurst. Be that as it may, in the two to three day span of time covered in *Come and Join the Dance* the main character, Susan Levitt:

—Breaks up with her earnest, hopelessly in love with her, but utterly clueless, boyfriend.
—Seeks the counsel of her best friend, Kay, who has dropped out of the Barnard-like college they'd been attending to move into a nearby residential hotel. Kay is the closest we get to a Beat woman in this book.
—Learns when she finally does check her mailbox, where she'd been letting her mail pile up for several weeks, that she is not going to get her diploma after all due to her failure to attend the requisite number of gym classes.
—Has her first two sexual encounters with two different men. One is an eighteen year old lost soul named Anthony; and the other is Kay's worldly, older-man boyfriend, Peter.
—Has to deal with her parents who come in from Cedarhurst, Long Island for her diploma-less graduation ceremony. The fact that blowing off a gym requirement denies Susan a diploma leaves her well-meaning father just plain bewildered that she could let such a thing happen, while

her proper, appearances-are-everything mother is just plain devastated.

While the above incidents sound like they could have been extracted from the text of a second rate (at best) soap opera, in the young Joyce Glassman's handling of them they make for a very moving story. Glassman's book came out right on the cusp of the political and cultural upheavals of 1960s but, in a manner similar to that of *On the Road*, it is based on happenings from nearly a decade prior—assuming, as I am, that it draws on the author's experiences at Barnard College in the early 1950s. While it tells a very different kind of story, and is written in a very different style, there is a similar flavor to *Come and Join the Dance* as there is in *On the Road*.

In each of these novels the central character, Susan Levitt/Sal Paradise, is reaching beyond her/himself for a missing dimension to life which s/he can only vaguely apprehend without knowing for sure if it is even there. Both Susan Levitt and Sal Paradise look to a companion and soul-mate, within whom they each see an embodiment of a dimension to life and living they each want and need for themselves. For Sal Paradise (Jack Kerouac) it is Dean Moriarty (Neal Cassady), and for Susan Levitt (Joyce Glassman) it is Kay (Elise Cowan). Each character also experiences the intertwining of a giddy kind of joy in breaking loose from convention with an equal element of sadness and loss that comes from not knowing if such breaking loose will really leave their lives in any kind of a better place—however "better" may be defined. And as Kerouac's Sal Paradise seeks his deliverance from convention in the company of the "mad ones," for Glassman's Susan it is those she brands as "outlaws" to whom she looks for inspiration and insight:

> She [Susan] had only felt at home in nondescript places...Kay had taught her what a significant thing is was to cut a class, not just an irresponsible act. Her parents, paying bills for "advantages we never had," would not understand, but stolen time had such a liveness to it; *you could really feel yourself exist* [emphasis added]...How long it had taken her to discover this! Peter, Kay, and Anthony...they were outlaws, part of a mysterious underground brotherhood. How was it that she had suddenly become able to recognize them...?

But my point and purpose here are not to indicate a few thematic similarities between *On the Road* and *Come and Join the Dance*. The characters in *On the Road*, who are on their quests of the spirit, and out to feel that they really exist, are—in the eyes of many readers of Kerouac—heroic. They are yet another incarnation of the prototype the late scholar of mythology, Dr. Joseph Campbell, describes in his well known work *The Hero's Journey*. But can a woman—particularly a white, middle-class woman in 1950s America—embark upon a hero, or heroine's, journey of her own and on her own terms? *Come and Join the Dance* ends before Susan embarks for Paris, and the reader is left not knowing for sure if she even goes. But, at the outset of the novel anyway, a planned trip to Paris is the closest she can come to her own journey of the spirit, because it is the only such journey that her culture and social standing will permit. What may have been regarded as heroic for males of that time—or, if not exactly heroic, at least an understandable and reasonably acceptable expression of male wanderlust and personal explora-tion—was often regarded in females as symptomatic or indicative of mental illness.

The late Beat poet Gregory Corso made precisely this point when a ques-tion arose at a Naropa Institute conference in 1994 about why there were so few Beat women writers. However exasperatingly off-the-wall Gregory could be at times, he offered a very cogent observation on this occasion:

> There were women, they were there, I knew them, their families put them in institutions, they were given electric shock. In the 50s if you were a male you could be a rebel, but if you were female your families had you locked up. There were cases, I knew them, someday someone will write about them.

While Corso may have been engaging in a little hyperbole there, which was his well known stock in trade, his larger point is quite valid.

Elise Cowan, the prototype for Glassman's Kay, is a case in point. She was a very intelligent and poetic individual, who actually did graduate from Barnard, and who was never quite able to find a place for herself in either New York or San Francisco following her Barnard years. She took typing jobs to pay the rent and buy the groceries while writing her poems—none of which were published in her lifetime. She fell deeply in love with Allen Ginsberg, but just at the time that he was coming to terms with his ho-mosexuality. After several hospitalizations, at the hands of her parents, for depression and paranoid fantasies, including a stay on Bellevue's psychiatric ward in New York City, Ms. Cowan committed suicide in 1962.

Were her depression, and her paranoid fantasies, organic to her nature or were they ultimately rooted in the ethos of a culture that offered practically no space or outlets for the kind of creative drive and spirit found in a young woman like Elise Cowan? I'm not a mental health expert. My best guess is that it was probably some of both. I also know that some very poetic and creative male writers of approximately the same time and genre—like Lew Welch and Richard Brautigan—also took their lives.

But Gregory Corso's larger point, I feel, still stands: It was far more dangerous for a young woman in the 1950s to embark upon a journey of the spirit, and upon a journey of self-discovery and self-awareness—to attempt to discover if she really existed or not, as Glassman's Susan Levitt put it—than it was for a man.

Still, some did. I found it illuminating to read poet Diane di Prima's recently published memoir, *Recollections of My Life as a Woman* (Penguin Books, 2001), as a companion piece to *Come and Join the Dance*, however unlikely such a pairing may initially seem. While she certainly had her dealings with some of the men of the Beat era—LeRoi Jones (now Amiri Baraka) in particular—di Prima is not identified with a particular male in the same way that many of the women of the Beat Generation are. She definitely did it her way. Di Prima's *Recollections of My Life as a Woman* is the real-life story of a real-life woman choosing to live the life that the fictitious Susan Levitt can only just barely imagine.

Diane di Prima dropped out Swarthmore College in 1953 and chose to make her own way in her native New York City. She was far from a child of privilege. Her family was working-class Italian and her grandparents were Italian emigrants. Her scholarship to Swarthmore was, in her parents' eyes, her ticket to mainstream American achievement and respectability; much in the same way that Jack Kerouac's French-Canadian immigrant parents regarded his scholarship to Columbia. Like Kerouac, di Prima handed back the ticket instead of cashing it in. Unlike Kerouac, however, di Prima has survived and thrived.

To hear Ms. di Prima, now in her early 70s, look back to what gave her the impetus to pursue the life she's lived is instructive. In an interview given to *Beat Scene* magazine in the mid-1990s she notes the positive influence her grandparents had on her ways of thinking and being—particularly her anarchist grandfather—but then goes on to say:

> As I've gotten older and gotten more in touch with what went on at home when I was young, part of it was just pure rage on my part, and a real need to get away from the home environment...and rather than going crazy, I became a writer.

The genesis of the rage to which di Prima refers here is in her immediate family—a physically abusive father and an often hysterical mother. Her contention that she became a writer as an alternative to going crazy herself is reflective of William Burroughs' assertion that his only way of dealing with his life-long "struggle with the Ugly Spirit" was to "write my way out."

But while di Prima is able to name a specific source for her rage, i.e. her family of origin, I'm going to be bold (or reckless) enough to speculate that she was/is also writing from, and tapping into, a more generalized kind of rage. It was a rage, I'll further speculate that went largely unrealized, unrecognized, and certainly unexpressed by any number of young women of her era. It was not a ranting, raving, hysterical kind of rage for the most part, but a rage borne out of not knowing if you really existed on your own terms or not. Granted, there is not even an allusion to Susan Levitt's experiencing any kind of overt rage in *Come and Join the Dance*, but her not knowing if she had any kind of authentic life she could truly call her own had to generate, on some level of her being, a well of anger.

Susan Levitt, of course, is a fictional character; but the existential condition she represented was very real for any reasonably aware young woman coming of age at that time and place. Diane di Prima was one such woman of that time. The rage from which she wrote, as her antidote to going crazy, I would offer, was both personal and cultural. Her determination to be her own person and to write her own truth took her down some pretty risky, and at times quite treacherous, roads. She often lived a hand-to- mouth existence—in both New York City and in the San Francisco Bay Area. She and LeRoi Jones founded their own small press outfit for a time in order to give like-minded writers and poets at least some small public voice since no mainstream press would touch them. She had five children from four different fathers, raising most of them without the father present. I don't know that di Prima would hold up the day-to-day and year-to-year doings of her life as a model to be emulated. She really has no need or reason to do so. She was mostly just trying to live for herself, make some kind of a living, and stand up for her friends and for those whom she cared about.

But, as Ginsberg said of Kerouac following Kerouac's death, Diane di Prima made a "crack in the consciousness." In her case it was a crack not only in the cultural consciousness as to the right and proper role of a woman in conventional society, but in a cultural consciousness that imposed a mind-lock, as it were, on imagined ways of living altogether. To actually set out to live the life one imagines—with all the attendant pitfalls that will inevitably come one's way in so doing—is a truly radical deed. It is a radical act of the spirit. It represents a willingness and a drive to deliberately live out the lines of an African-American spiritual: "I'm Going to Do What The Spirit Say Do." For di Prima, living by these words was not even a choice so much as it was/is a spiritual imperative.

Diane di Prima took up the spiritual battle—or joined the dance, if you will—at a very young age, and is still at it. In her later years her spiritual path took her to Tibetan Buddhism, and to some teaching opportunities at the San Francisco Institute of Magickal and Healing Arts.

Early on in this chapter I said I would only focus on a few of the Beat women writers in any extensive way, and this has been the case. But, in addition to those already mentioned, tribute at least needs to be paid to such poets and novelists as Joanne Kyger, Lenore Kandel, Brenda Frazer, Joanna McClure, Janine Pommy Vega, ruth weiss, and Jan Kerouac. Some of the chroniclers of that era also certainly deserve tribute, women like Hettie Cohen Jones, Joan Haverty, and Eileen Kaufman. All of these gifted women brought the fruits of the Spirit of Life to their readers.

One of the more gifted and insightful chroniclers of the Beat era is Carolyn Robinson Cassady. She offers her twenty-plus year perspective on the West Coast Beat scene in her work that was referenced in the previous chapter, *Off the Road—My Years with Cassady, Kerouac, and Ginsberg* (Penguin Books, 1990). The insights she offers into the life of her husband of 16 years, Neal Cassady, as well as the lives of Jack Kerouac and Allen Ginsberg, bring a wealth of information and understanding to the larger

Beat movement that would have otherwise gone unrecorded.

In more recent times Ms. Cassady has been instrumental in bringing forth the publication of Neal Cassady's *Collected Letters, 1944-1967*, edited by Dave Moore (Penguin Books, 2004). Among many other things, these letters demonstrate, through the voluminous correspondences of both Neal and Carolyn Cassady, that they were each accomplished writers in their own right. As one who has been privileged to view some of her paintings, I can also attest to the fact that Carolyn Cassady is a gifted artist. She continues to offer guidance and inspiration to those today who continue to seek greater understanding of the Beats.

I said at the outset that this was the chapter I felt least equipped to write. Nothing I've subsequently written has changed my mind in that regard. When it comes to bearing witness to a female spiritual consciousness that a good number of women writers brought to the Beat movement, I still feel as if I'm looking through a window rather than being in the room with it.

Maybe that's as close as I, or any man, can get.

CHAPTER ELEVEN

Gerard Kerouac, The Buddha, and Jesus Christ

The St. Louis de Gonzague Cemetery in Nashua, New Hampshire is about a five minute drive from my home. It opened in 1880, shortly after the St. Louis de Gonzague Roman Catholic Church was founded in Nashua for the newly arriving French-Canadian immigrants. Among those new arrivals who purchased a family plot in this cemetery was Jack Kerouac's paternal grandfather, Jean Baptiste Kerouac of St. Hubert, Quebec. Jean Baptiste had no way of knowing, of course, that the plot he purchased would come to be the locale for the closing chapters in three of the novels his grandson would later write. The three novels are *The Town and the City, Visions of Gerard,* and *Vanity of Duluoz.* Jean Baptiste, in fact, never even knew his grandson, Jean Louis "Jack" Kerouac, since he was born 16 years after his grandfather had died.

This Kerouac grave site is one of my personally sacred places to which I feel drawn periodically. Sometimes in my comings and goings around Nashua I'll stop by this spot as a way of centering myself. The plot in which Gerard is buried is also the burial site for his, and Jack's parents, Leo and Gabrielle Kerouac. In 1997 the ashes of Jack Kerouac's daughter, Jan Michele Kerouac, were also interred here. The current marker was put in place by Stella Sampas Kerouac, Jack's third wife, following the death of Gabrielle in 1973.

When I visit this gravesite, I often reflect on how the death of a nine-year-old boy in 1926 affected not only the life of his younger brother, but how the life and death of Gerard Kerouac has touched countless persons around the world when they read *Visions of Gerard.* I'll even confess to this: Sometimes on a rainy or snowy New England night when the driving gets a little dicey, and if my route home takes me past this cemetery, I'll offer up a short prayer to "Saint Gerard" to get me to the safety of my street and house. I'm not a Catholic. I'm even a skeptic when it comes to the value, and workability, of intercessory prayer. Nonetheless I feel drawn to seek the assistance of a long dead nine-year-old. And it has gotten me home safely every time!

When I lead tours of Nashua for the annual Kerouac festival in October I read, while standing by this grave, the concluding paragraphs of *The Town and the City* and *Vanity of Duluoz,* the first and last novels, respectively, that Kerouac wrote and saw published in his lifetime. These paragraphs, in each of these works, describe the burial of Jack's father, Leo—as George Martin and Emil Duluoz. But it is the closing paragraphs of *Visions of Gerard* that carry the most power when read at this site. In them Jack Kerouac recalls the funeral procession for Gerard when the writer was four years old, and was called Ti Jean:

> We all get in cars and they slowly weave the parade and out we go on a long slow drive along the Merrimack River…to the bridge at Tyngsboro, and across that to Nashua (my parents come-from town) in bleak array to the cemetery outside of town…and they haul the coffin gently down to the grave ropes…

I've had Kerouac aficionados and scholars from all over America, Canada, and various parts of the world present with me when I read these words. In a way reminiscent of Mike in an earlier chapter, I've witnessed some pretty emotional moments in the course of my reading. Some of my tour-takers want to re-live what is being described. They look for the "long gray wall and the glistening boulevard in the rain" that Kerouac described. Often someone will place his or her hand on the marker that bears Gerard's name in the way that one might touch a holy shrine. Some will say a prayer, or just stand in silence. Occasionally tears are shed. And all of this because of a book Jack Kerouac wrote some 30 years after his older brother's tragic childhood death from rheumatic fever.

How to account for all this? Gerard Kerouac's death, tragic and grief-laden as it was, was no more so than countless other childhood deaths that parents and families have had to mourn over the course of human history. Many childhood diseases, now treatable as a matter of routine, claimed the lives of countless little boys and girls in decades and centuries past—both in this country and around the world. The short life of Gerard Kerouac of Lowell, Massachusetts just happened to be one of them. But Gerard's life and death came to be held up in a way that transcended and transfigured his brief, and rather ordinary, earthly existence. In the eyes and through the words of his younger brother Gerard became a mythic figure. He became both the embodiment, or incarnation, of the innocence of childhood, as well as a representation of the tissue-thin fragility of life. Writing out of his own spiritual angst Jack Kerouac imparts to his older, yet long deceased, brother a kind of divinity. Gerard's divinity is universal It is one expression of what Ralph Waldo Emerson called "the spark of the Divine" that is contained within each and all of us. To take it one step further, the deification of Gerard Kerouac is roughly analogous to what happened to another obscure figure, Jesus of Nazareth, following his death some two millennia ago.

But I'm getting ahead of myself. Let's stick with the earthly Gerard and the earthly Kerouacs of 1920s Lowell for awhile. They have their own story after all. It's the story of hundreds of other French-Canadian families living in the mill towns of New England at that time. Leo Kerouac and Gabrielle Levesque Kerouac were the children of immigrants, brought from Quebec to the United States in their infancy. They met and married in Nashua, New Hampshire. A job offer for Leo took them to Lowell. By the French-Canadian, or Franco-American, Catholic standards of their day their family of three children was small: Gerard, Caroline, and their youngest son, Jean Louis.

At some point it became clear that something wasn't quite right with Gerard. He had trouble breathing; his legs ached a lot; and he spent more and more time bedridden. He had a disease called rheumatic fever, for which there was no cure at that time. In June of 1926, after a prolonged period of agonized suffering, Gerard died before reaching his tenth birthday. His sister Caroline was seven years old and his younger brother, Jean Louis, Ti Jean, was four. Gerard's Funeral Mass was held in Lowell at the St. Louis de France Church where he and his brother Jack were baptized, but his body was taken to the Kerouac family plot in Nashua for burial.

In this devoutly Catholic household Gerard may have been gone but he was anything but forgotten. In a way reminiscent of the designation of sainthood by the Catholic Church, a beatification process of Gerard took place within the Kerouac family. His goodness, his kindly ways, his love of animals, and his devotion to his parents were recalled as the stories of the saintly Gerard were told and retold. He nursed a crippled mouse to health only to be devastated when the little creature was eaten by the family cat. He braved the elements of a cold Lowell night to walk to a neighborhood drugstore for aspirin for his mother's severe headache. These kinds of Gerard Stories became part of the Kerouac family lore; and the person most affected by them was the youngster, Ti Jean.

By the time this youngster got to junior high school he'd become Jack Kerouac to his friends. He was handsome, athletic, and had a decidedly poetic and literary bent about him. He clearly had the potential to move out of and beyond the mill town neighborhoods that his parents and grandparents knew. But he also struggled throughout his boyhood, adolescence, and into his adulthood with the legacy of this absent, and yet powerfully present, older brother. A deeply sensitive soul, Jack spent much of his life struggling to find some meaning or some rationale for the existence of suffering and death. At times this struggle became an obsession. Gerard became his paradigm for the needless suffering of the innocents.

There was also a pronounced element of guilt as Jack learned the legacy of Gerard. Today it would be called "survivor guilt." Why Gerard and not me? How come I get to live out my life while he was denied his? In many instances Gerard became the standard against which Jack was measured within his family. How is a mere mortal supposed to measure up against a beatified saint? It was a stacked deck with Jack always coming out as the inadequate one. This guilt was further compounded by Kerouac's awareness, as he moved into adulthood, that, as a child, he'd once wished Gerard dead.

In March of 1945, as his Beat circle of friends was coming together in New York City, Jack wrote a letter to his sister Caroline about some analysis he'd been undergoing. While not specified, the "analyst" was probably

William Burroughs, who had a strong interest in psychiatry but did not become an official practitioner. In this letter Jack acknowledges to his sister that his only actual conscious memory of Gerard was of a time when they were playing, and in response to some kind of sibling conflict that developed "Saint Gerard" slapped his little brother in the face. The stunned and angry Ti Jean, in that moment, wished his older brother dead, without fully comprehending, most likely, what death actually meant. So, as Jack explained to Caroline, he'd been subconsciously punishing himself all these years for willing the death of his older brother, which was why (he thought) his life had already hit several dead ends. Jack goes on to say that what he really needs to do is try to remember the good and kind things about Gerard as a way of offsetting this destructive guilt he's been carrying around. (*Selected Letters—Jack Kerouac 1940-1956.* Ann Charters, Editor. Viking, 1995).

Eleven years after writing this letter to his sister, in January of 1956, Jack set out to do just that, remember the good and kind things about Gerard. Interestingly enough, it was at his sister's home in Rocky Mount, North Carolina where she was living with her husband, their son, and mother Gabrielle, that Jack wrote *Visions of Gerard.* He'd written the genesis of the book about five years earlier in a series of letters to Neal Cassady in which he poured forth to his soul-mate the effect Gerard's death had on him. Before looking at Kerouac in Rocky Mount in the early weeks of 1956, however, a bird's eye view of his life at that time would be in order.

The year 1956 was a pivotal one in Kerouac's career life as well as with his spiritual journey. Things were finally beginning to move with Viking Press and it looked like *On the Road* would indeed be published. By now he'd already written the bulk of what would eventually become his published works. The years 1955-56 also represented the height of Kerouac's Buddhist phase. In the fall of '55, on a trip to the San Francisco Bay area, Kerouac caught the San Francisco Renaissance, which has been described in previous chapters, as it kicked into high gear. Kerouac and Gary Snyder, along with John Montgomery, climbed Matterhorn Peak in Yosemite National Park that fall. It was through Snyder that Kerouac learned of fire lookout job on Washington State's Desolation Peak for which he applies for the summer of '56. This literal and figurative mountain-top experience is described in *The Dharma Bums and in Desolation Angels.*

It was also in Gary Snyder that Kerouac found someone with whom he could share in depth his attraction to Buddhism, although they each came at Buddhism in different ways. Synder, for example, was not bringing the weight of conservative Catholic baggage with him. Jack had discovered Buddhism a couple of years earlier, but it was through his conversations with Snyder that his Buddhism was both refined and challenged. So, for a certain period of his life—unfortunately it didn't last throughout his life—Kerouac found in the Four Noble Truths of Buddhism a way of dealing with his near obsession with human suffering; an obsession rooted at least in part in the suffering and death of Gerard. These Four Truths have been expressed in many ways. Without, I hope, trivializing them, here's my own way of stating them: 1. Suffering happens because life happens. 2. We suffer because we desire that life be more than it is. 3. We relinquish suffering by letting go of this desire that life be something other than what it is. 4. Such relinquishment is accomplished by following the Eight Fold Path.

An explication of the Eight Fold Path is beyond the scope of this chapter other than to say that it involves such things as right thought, right action, right mindfulness, and right concentration. It is traveled by practicing, among other things, acts of kindness and mercy in one's day to day life, and by engaging in certain meditative practices. The eventual goal of the Eight Fold Path is the release from our pain, which is brought on by undue attachment to all that is temporal, and a union with the eternal, in which we realize who we really are. The teachings of the Buddha, as well as the teachings of Jesus of Nazareth, offer guideposts for following this path. It was this goal of release from the temporal and union with the eternal that was the object of Kerouac's spiritual striving as he set out to write *Visions of Gerard*.

For those first three weeks of 1956 Kerouac had the Rocky Mount house to himself as the rest of the family was away. He had a little meditation area in the woods behind the house, and a writing area on the porch. In the opening paragraph of the book he began writing there, he stated: "For the first four years of my life I was not Ti Jean, I was Gerard...and his holiness and his teachings of tenderness to me, and my mother, constantly remind me to pay attention to his goodness and advice." Kerouac's Catholicism—which, for all his battles with it, he never forsook—and his attraction to Buddhism come together in *Visions of Gerard*. The kindness and the gentleness he attributes to his long dead brother mirror some of the traits called for if one is to right-fully follow the Eight Fold Path. Consciously or not, in some places Kerouac made Gerard into a little Buddhist. Consider this passage:

> Today his mind is perplexed and he looks up into the perfect cloud-less empty blue and wonders what all the bruiting and furor is below, what all the yelling, the buildings, the humanity, the concern—'Maybe there is nothing at all,' he divines in his lucid pureness—'Just like the smoke that comes out of Papa's pipe'—'All I gotta do is close my eyes and it all goes away—'There *is* no Mama, no Ti Jean, no Ti Nin, no Papa—no me—no *kitigi*' (the cat)—'There is no earth—look at the perfect sky, it says nothing.'

What Kerouac describes here is the attainment of the Buddhist ideal of the awareness of, quite literally, "no thing"; the letting of all that is temporal ("Maybe there is nothing at all") and a joining with that which is beyond the temporal—"Look at the perfect sky, it says nothing." Kerouac is making his brother his spirit guide for following the Eight Fold Path. Gerard, one might say, became his Buddha.

At the same time Gerard also became Kerouac's Christ. In *Visions of Gerad* Kerouac is attempting a meld, if you will, of Catholicism and Buddhism, as he has known and experienced each. (He also attempted to come to terms with, and make his peace with, his French-Canadian lineage, but that's another matter.) Thirty years after Gerard's death, his living brother wrote about the life of one who, within their family matrix, became the Ideal Child, and the Ideal Human Being, as his memory was revered.

Gerard, that is to say, became mythologized as Jack drew on the Gerard lore he'd heard all his life. As told by Kerouac: Gerard had visions of heaven that he related to the nuns at the Catholic school he attended. He made his confession in such a way that left the confessor/priest thinking that Gerard himself would be a priest, i.e. a representative of Christ on Earth, someday. His kindly ways were remembered and related over and over just as Jack had told Caroline he needed to do in that March, 1945 letter.

But Gerard didn't achieve the priesthood. He died instead after a period of prolonged suffering. His death was mourned. He was carried to his grave. And then, within the Kerouac household this dead child became resurrected, as is were, as the Legend of Gerard went forth. As a way of redeeming himself from his sense of guilt from wishing for Gerard's death, Jack beatified his older brother.

In researching my previous book on Jack Kerouac's extended family I was fortunate enough to interview a couple of elderly gentlemen—one of whom was Gerard's first cousin—who knew Gerard when they were all youngsters in Lowell. What these gentlemen recalled was that Gerard was just one of your basic neighborhood kids who had the tragic misfortune of coming down with an illness that killed him. He was a nice enough guy, they remembered, who did a lot of the usual kid stuff, and got into a lot of the usual kid mischief that children of that time and place did. As for his being a saint, or a little god, well, as one of his one-time playmates put it, "I thought he was just a good kid."

So how true, then, is the Legend of Gerard as Jack told it? Was he really some combination of Christ and Buddha? Or is this one of those cases where truth is not necessarily identical with fact? To get at this point, let's consider how another legend was once made. This one initially took shape some two thousand years ago in an obscure Middle East land.

An itinerant Jewish teacher of that time and place, from his society's peasant/working class, traveled the countryside offering a rather simple message of love, compassion, and justice based on his knowledge of Jewish scripture. He proclaimed an approaching "Kingdom of God" as he called it. The Realm of the Sacred would be an apt translation today. He performed acts of love and kindness and healing, and drew a following unto himself. This was at a time when a number of itinerant teachers and self-proclaimed messiahs of one type or another were preaching some form of deliverance to any who would listen to them. But this particular teacher and preacher, with the not uncommon name of Jesus, had the misfortune of running afoul of the religious and political leaders of his day. They feared anyone who was gaining a popular following which could lead to a popular uprising. So they had the teacher, Jesus, executed; and, according to the legend, it was a slow, agonized, and painful death.

End of story? Not quite. Within his circle of followers—his earthly family one might say—Jesus became the Ideal, the Perfect Human Being, so much so that he was even called the Son of God. Within this family, which began to expand and spin off other families (churches as they came to be called) the Legend of Jesus grew. There were stories of how he healed the sick, and caused the blind to recover their sight; and on one occasion he even raised a man from the dead. Jesus became the compassionate one, the friend of the poor and the downtrodden, as well as the one who was unafraid to speak truth to power even though it costs him his life. These Jesus Stories became part of the lore of this slowly expanding community that revered his life and memory. As some of the leaders and theologians in this community told their Jesus Stories, his death became redemptive. They said he died in order that others might live, and that believers might therefore strive to live the life Jesus exemplified. Beginning some 30 years after the death of the earthly Jesus, his Legend was written down by several people, in a variety of versions, and the earthly Jesus became mythologized as The Christ—even The Christ whom death itself could not conquer as he arose from the dead.

Jack Kerouac, as the author of *Visions of Gerard*, and the writers of what eventually became the New Testament Gospels, performed essentially the same function. They took an earthly human being and elevated him to the realm of divinity. I'm aware that any analogy can only go so far. We know who the earthly Gerard actually was. I've spoken with folk who knew him. His birth, baptismal certificate, and death certificate all exist. The house in Lowell in which he lived and died is still standing, and people live in it today. While I can't dig him up I can show you where his body is.

With Jesus we're dealing with a much more shadowy figure, a quasi-historical person. He cannot be identified in the same way that the earthly, human Gerard Kerouac can. But the process by which an earthly human being became, in a very real sense, deified, has its similarities in each case. And what we know about Gerard and Jesus, and the Buddha as well for that matter, is contained in the stories that came to be told about them and their earthly actions.

Here's my point: We have, in essence, two Gerards and two Jesuses here. We have the earthly beings, and the creations of *Visions of Gerard* and the New Testament Gospels respectively. Which figure, with respect to both Gerard and Jesus is more real? Which figure has blessed and touched more lives? Which figure is more "true"? The truth of great literature—and I'm treating the New Testament as literature here—lies more in how it touches our lives, and in what it tells us about ourselves, than in how factually correct it is. The truth of *Visions of Gerard* and the truth of the New Testament Gospels are both, therefore, the truths of myth.

The truths of myth? Yes, and here's how I see that truth played out in *Visions of Gerard*. While Kerouac's novel, unlike the New Testament, contains no resurrection legend, the novel itself is a resurrection of a beatified and holy Gerard. This is the Gerard who draws people to the novel that bears his name, and that bring them to his one-time home, and to his grave. The Gerard Kerouac of *Visions of Gerard* represents the idealism, the innocence, the goodness, the promises, and the dreams that are universally associated with young children because he is the child forever frozen in time as a nine year old. The Gerard that Kerouac gave us also represents the Holiness and the Sacredness of Life itself. The holiness that Jack Kerouac located in his brother is reflective of the aforementioned Emersonian "spark of the D
ivine" that resides in all of us. In holding up this kind of holiness, which is discoverable in each one of us, Kerouac performs the role of a spirit guide.

In a similar way, the mythologized Jesus, who is found in the New Testament, is one who exemplifies a person who was deeply in touch with his essential humanity, and also in touch with his innate divinity or holiness, in a way that few persons who have ever lived on this planet are. The Buddha was another such individual. The Jesus figure of the Gospels represents the most positive reaches of human possibility when it comes to being a compassionate, healing, and justice-loving person. Jesus' message, as I have come to understand it for myself, was/is that "my life is your life." For all this person/figure had to say about the Kingdom of God, his message, as I see it, came down to one essential point when he said, "The Kingdom of God—or the Realm of the Sacred—is *within you*" (emphasis added).

I believe Jack Kerouac was seeking to do several things when he set out to write *Visions of Gerard*. He was, as previously noted, trying to make peace with his French-Canadian origins and ancestry. He wanted to make peace with his extended family. His parents, aunts, uncles, and cousins are given more extensive treatment in this novel than in any other single piece of Kerouac's work. He was reconciling, if possible, the Roman Catholicism in which he'd been raised, and to which he still felt some allegiance, with the Buddhism he'd immersed himself in by 1956. He attributed a number of

Buddhist qualities to Gerard while also saying, "I'll never malign the church that gave Gerard a blessed baptism, nor the hand that waved over his grave and officially dedicated it."

While he was not a scholar of comparative religion, Kerouac at least points to an underlying unity in religion as he discovers some of the same essence at the heart of Buddhism and Christianity. In writing *The Dharma Bums,* two years after *Visions of Gerard,* Kerouac would make reference to "the truth that is realizable in a dead man's bones and is beyond the Tree of Buddha as well as the Cross of Jesus. *Believe* the world is an ethereal flower, and ye live."

Above all, in those early weeks of 1956 thirty-year old Jack Kerouac was attempting to come to terms with a shadowy presence that had both haunted and blessed him throughout his life. He wanted to come to terms with both the death of his older brother as well as the beatified life that his brother continued to have beyond the grave. His mythologizing of Gerard was not a falsification, but rather a celebration of the human possibility that dwells in all of us. The true function of religion, and of a spirit guide, is to awaken the spirit and awaken the soul. In *Visions of Gerard* Kerouac was trying to awaken himself, Buddhist style, to the meaning of his older brother's life and death. In so doing he also performed a religious task for his readers in awakening us to the Holiness of Life itself.

CHAPTER TWELVE

Who Am I, On This Lilac Evening?

One of my more memorable events of the year 2004 was attending the opening program for an exhibition of the original manuscript of *On the Road* at Marquette University in Milwaukee, Wisconsin. I had a conversation there with an English professor at Marquette named Angela Sorby. She led an ongoing discussion series in conjunction with the scroll exhibit. We sat just a few feet away from the forty-foot long case in which the manuscript was displayed as we talked about the novel's enduring significance. Professor Sorby offered this observation:

> *On the Road* is a college novel in a way. The GI Bill in the late 1940s let so many people go to college (in a way that had not been the case previously). Everybody who goes to college wants to have that road experience. I think it is a phenomenon of post World War II America that people in college want to escape the identity they've been given—class, race, etc. and experiment. *On the Road* speaks well to that experience.

Angela's point is well taken. I would only expand upon it a bit to say that *On the Road* is a classic, coming-of-age novel—whether one attends college or not—in that it speaks to that universal experience of having to define oneself both in relation to, as well as counter to, one's upbringing, with all that that upbringing contains. While the exterior landscape of *On the Road* is the geography of America in the late 1940s, the interior landscape is the soul of Sal Paradise as he struggles with the question we all encounter in our coming-of-age years: Who am I?

Recall again Professor Sorby's words about how persons of a certain age "want to escape the identity they've been given—class, race, etc. and experiment," and place them along side this paragraph from *On the Road:*

> At lilac evening I walked with every muscle aching in the Denver colored section, wishing I were a Negro, feeling that the best the white world had offered was not enough ecstasy for me, not enough life, joy, kicks, darkness, music, not enough night. I stopped in at a little shack where a man sold red hot chili in paper containers; I bought some and ate it, strolling in the dark mysterious streets. I wished I were a Denver Mexican, or even a poor overworked Jap, anything but what I was so drearily, a "white man" disillusioned. All my life I'd had white ambitions; that was why I'd abandoned a good woman like Terry in the San Joachin Valley. I passed the dark porches of Mexican and Negro homes…A gang of colored women came by, and one of the young ones detached herself from motherlike elders and came to me fast—"Hello Joe"—and suddenly she saw it wasn't Joe and ran back, blushing. I was only myself, Sal Paradise, sad, strolling in this violet dark, this unbearably sweet night, wishing I could exchange worlds with the happy, true-hearted, ecstatic Negroes of America.

Kerouac was much taken to task for these words in the aftermath of the publication of *On the Road*. Taken on their own, his sentiments can easily come off as an expression of nothing more than romanticized racism on the part of a hopelessly naïve wannabe-black white guy. Indeed this was the charge leveled by one of Kerouac's most caustic critics, *Commentary* magazine editor, Norman Podhoretz, who noted in an essay shortly after *On the Road*'s publication that it would certainly come as news to the "Negroes of America," circa 1949, that they were "happy, true-hearted, and ecstatic."

Taken strictly on its own, Podhoretz's point certainly has truth to it. But his put-down of Kerouac was contained within a sneering, look-down-the-nose essay called *The Know-Nothing Bohemians,* in which Podhoretz accused Kerouac and his Beat Generation contemporaries of being the avowed enemies of all that was right, good, proper, and decent about civilized America in the 1950s. In a way Podhoretz was reflecting a wider cultural attitude about the Beats themselves in his article. But while the Beats have gained a wider measure of understanding, acceptance and even respectability over the past several decades, Norman Podhoretz has continued to visit his sneer upon them. One would think he'd get over it at some point, but one would be wrong.

Let's return to Kerouac and his lilac evening in Denver in the spring of 1949. Yes, to read those disillusioned words of his in light of all we know about racial matters in America in the ensuing half-century since they were written is to feel a twinge—perhaps it's more than just a twinge—of embarrassment for the author. But this is one of those cases where, for all the magical things Kerouac could do with words, you have to both read, and then read past, his words in order to get at what he's actually saying. First I would suggest that you read them as you think about the America of 1949. Read this passage while reflecting upon an America whose white population preferred to forget about the black and brown men and women who had served their country—and many who lost their lives—just a few years earlier in World War II. Read it as you think of an America who wanted to relegate its people of color back to their invisibility, if not their non-personhood, of the pre-World War II era.

At approximately the same time, in fact, that Kerouac took his stroll through this "colored section" as he called it, William Levitt was literally shaping and designing both the physical and cultural landscape of post-World War II America by building the country's first cookie-cutter suburb in Levittown, Long Island, New York. As a telling indicator of the place and status of people of color in the United States, as it was getting back to normal following the War, look at these stark words found in the agreement that returning American GIs had to sign as they bought their homes in Levittown for $100.00 down: "The tenant agrees not to permit the premises to be used or occupied by any person other than members of the Caucasian race." Getting back to normal apparently included getting back to the "normal" quantity of racism that permeated the United States prior to the War.

Read this passage as you think about the author who was portraying himself as a character named Sal Paradise. In 1949 Jack Kerouac was a 27 year old man, still trying to figure out who he was, and where his niche in life would be. He was far from resolved on the matter. Walking through this so-called "colored section" of Denver, Jack was aware that he had grown up in an ethnic section himself in Lowell, Massachusetts, in one of its French-

Canadian enclaves. He grew up aware of a dominant culture to which he and his family did not belong. He did not even speak the language of this dominant culture until he was six years old.

More telling, several years prior to that night in Denver, Kerouac had, in effect, handed back the ticket that would very likely have given him entrée into the dominant white, well-educated, economically secure culture of his day when he walked away from Columbia University. When, in the fall of 1942, Kerouac dropped out of Columbia—thereby forfeiting his football scholarship—there was considerably more going on, I believe, than a dispute with his football coach over his lack of playing time. Perhaps it was an unconscious decision, but in leaving Columbia's prestigious arena, Jack was also returning his ticket of admission to the respectable, upwardly mobile, career-oriented (if one was male), white, suburban America of the 1950s. A degree from one of the country's most prestigious universities would have clearly given him entry to such a world. He greatly disappointed, and angered, his parents with this move, as their son's admission to Columbia represented the fulfillment of practically every immigrant's dream—that they would work and struggle so their children could, as the saying goes, "make good in America."

Kerouac places this immigrant's dream in the mind of his mother in a passage from *Maggie Cassidy*, which he wrote in 1953, as he described Gabrielle Kerouac's thoughts as her son set off for college in New York: "My mother was positive in her secret heart that I was to become a big executive of insurance companies. Just like when I made my First Confession, I was a little angel of pure future." Gabrielle's aspirations were not to be. At age 27 her "angel of pure future" was nowhere near the office of an insurance executive. He was instead walking the down and out streets of Denver, still trying to figure out where he belonged.

Jack rejected the Columbia campus, along with all the future possibilities it might have afforded him. In looking for a milieu wherein he could discover who he was, Kerouac chose to be among the fringe, and sometimes outlaw folk of New York's Times Square, or among those who frequented the jazz clubs of Harlem.

In seeking his identity Kerouac chose to conduct his search among those who lived at the margins of society. Among the various meanings of the term Beat, as we have seen, was one that referred to those who were beaten down by society, or beaten out to the edges of mainstream society. This certainly included the non-white cultures. Perhaps Kerouac felt like this was the stance from which he could best pursue this matter of self-identity. This kind of Beatness—of not quite being in step—is as much a spiritual condition as anything else. While the term Beat often encompassed social or economic or cultural estrangement, it primarily referred to spiritual estrangement or alienation. Whether or not those among Denver's African-American population felt spiritually alienated in their personal lives, this was Kerouac's condition as he walked among them in the spring of 1949.

As previously stated, when Kerouac coined the term Beat Generation in 1948, he and John Clellon Holmes, were referring to all who shared this sense of estrangement. When Jack wrote of his feelings about how "the best the white world had (to offer) was not enough ecstasy for me, not enough life, joy, kicks, darkness, music, not enough night..." he was, I feel, not primarily making a literal racial reference with the term "white world." He was searching for a way of saying that he could not find any kind of personal fulfillment in the dominant culture of his day with its white institutions and attitudes. What comes off, in reading those words today, as a naïve romanticization of African-Americans (a term not used at that time), is Kerouac projecting his own spiritual needs onto an alternative subculture about which he actually knows very little, but with which he seeks an identity. What Kerouac is giving voice to is a gut level awareness that he feels a greater affinity and identity with those on the edges of society than with those who are cruising along in the mainstream.

Kerouac is engaged, at bottom, in a religious struggle. Similar to Kerouac's questions, in theologian Michael Novak's book *Ascent of the Mountain; Flight of the Dove*, Mr. Novak maintains that the two fundamental religious questions are "Who Am I?" and "Who are we—we under these stars?" Discovering who we are, and how we are related—related to ourselves, to the rest of humanity, to Life Itself, and to whatever Force, Power, Being (i.e. God) that we sense or believe is greater than ourselves—is the essence of the religious and spiritual journey. As Jack Kerouac, in the persona of Sal Paradise, took that walk in Denver's lilac evening he was taking one of the many steps and roads he would travel on his journey of meaning and spirit.

For Jack it was a very bumpy journey; and one that tragically never found its full fruition. While he felt genuinely drawn to those he called the "fellaheen," i.e. those who struggled to live on the margins of society, he also discovered that he could not fully engage himself with them and the ways in which they lived. He could be with them, but ultimately he could not be one of them. This was the lesson he'd learned at an earlier point in his *On the Road* chronicle. His line in the passage cited above about how he had "abandoned a good woman like Terry in the San Joachin Valley" refers to a brief fling he'd had with a young Hispanic woman a couple of years prior to his Denver walk.

Sal meets Terry (real name: Bea Franco) on a bus trip from San Francisco to Los Angeles on his first cross country venture. They go from necking on the bus, to finding a hotel room in Los Angeles, to Sal moving in with Terry and her son in the town of "Sabinal" (Selma), California, which is well to the north of L.A. Terry and her family are Mexican laborers. Sal, Terry, and Terry's young son pick cotton for $3.00 per one hundred pounds picked. For a few days Paradise/Kerouac thinks he's finally found Paradise. As the Shakers put it their well-known hymn, Sal feels as if he has "come down where one ought to be." He says: "My back began to ache. But it was beautiful kneeling and hiding in that earth. If I felt like resting I did, with my face on the pillow of the brown, moist earth. Birds sang an accompaniment. I thought I'd found my life's work."

When Sal learns that some "Okies…tied a man [presumably Mexican] to a tree and beat him to a pulp, " he takes some precautions of his own. "From then on I carried a big stick with me in the tent in case they got the idea *we Mexicans* [emphasis added] were fouling up their trailer camp. They thought I was a Mexican of course; and in a way, I am."

But in a much more pronounced way, Kerouac wasn't; his reference to "we Mexicans" notwithstanding. In time his aching back became more of an issue for him than the moist brown earth. He quickly discovered that Terry's little boy could pick cotton faster and more efficiently than he could. Then October came, and with it Jack's reminder to himself that "everyone goes home in October." And where, in this case, was home? It was Ozone Park, in Queens, New York, where his mother lived following the death of his father a little over a year earlier. While Kerouac may have wished he were a Negro, or fancied himself a Mexican, his home was in neither setting. Sal and Terry make vague plans to meet in New York, even though both of them know it will never happen. Jack Kerouac, as Sal Paradise, walks away from his abbreviated life as a Mexican with the words, "Well, lackaday, I was on the road again."

Who am I? Who are we, under these stars? Like much in both Jack Kerouac's life and writings there is a double-edged message to be found in his struggle with these fundamental questions. As we strive to create and establish an identity that is uniquely our own, we are not completely tied to the social and cultural setting into which we were born; and neither do we completely escape it. Just as we have to live within the paradox of needing both security and freedom, we also have to live in the tension between the identity we're given and the one towards which we aspire. Living within that tension is part of the spiritual journey.

Another crucial piece of one's spiritual journey involves making peace with where we have come from; making peace with our past; and making peace with the givens in our lives. By givens I mean the family that gave us birth, the setting in which we were raised, and the race, gender, sexual orientation, culture, and station in life that were handed us when we first took a breath on this planet. By make peace, I do not mean passively accept. I mean instead to acknowledge and affirm—again, as best we can—the givens about who we are, and then move on to build an identity of our own.

The mistake Kerouac makes, as reflected in *On the Road*, is that he seems to feel that in order to acquire an authentic identity for himself he has to become someone or something other than who he is. Yes, there was a part of Jack Kerouac that could make an authentic connection with those with whom he wished to identify: "I wished I were a Negro"..."we Mexicans..." But at the same time he cannot completely empty himself into someone else's life and world. His disillusionment, I would suggest, is not really in his being a white man, but rather it is his frustration in feeling that in order to reach beyond his white self he has to deny that self. He gets caught in a breach. He is reaching for an identity which, in the end, he cannot fully possess.

This was only one of the many struggles of the soul and spirit in which Jack Kerouac engaged throughout his life. And in that very struggle he takes on the role of a spirit guide. He gave us his life, and he gave us the accounts of his life, in order that we may see both the joys that can be found, and the demons that can be encountered, as we each pursue the Who am I? and Who are We? questions for ourselves.

We should not overlook the beauty, the poignancy, and the foresight that came out of that breach and out of Kerouac's struggle within it. At a time when most of white America wanted to keep its African American population in the Jim Crow condition of pre-World War II, Jack saw a life and a vibrancy in that population that would not remain suppressed or oppressed for much longer. Just few years later Martin Luther King evoked that life and vibrancy in shaping the civil rights movement, and Malcolm X evoked it in the name of African-American empowerment. At a time when most white Americans did not know of, much less see, the labor of the brown hands and brown backs that put food on their tables and clothes on their bodies, Jack Kerouac, if only for a brief time, took part in such labor himself. Nearly two decades after Jack Kerouac and Bea Franco worked the fields of central California, those brown hands and backs and bodies and souls—along with those of whites, Asians, and Native Americans—would be accorded a measure of hope and dignity and respect due to the organizing efforts of Caesar Chavez.

It was not until the late 1960s that white America was told that "Black is beautiful" and that "Brown is beautiful." Jack Kerouac had known and seen that some 20 years earlier. He may have taken the wrong track in trying to determine who he was, but the young Jack Kerouac at least had the eyes to see and the ears to hear those who Ralph Ellison had collectively described as *The Invisible Man.*

Those who are familiar with Kerouac's life know of the tragic turn it took in his later years. It was his abuse of alcohol, among other things, that drove him back into some of the provinciality in which he had been raised. By the time those with whom Jack had felt an affinity in the late 1940s began to find their voices and shake off their invisibility, Kerouac was no longer much interested in "life, joy, (and) kicks."

We should honor his life, nonetheless. We should honor, we should in fact praise, Jack Kerouac's willingness, and his courage, to push the "Who am I?" question as far as he did. We should honor his efforts to possess for himself something of what he saw and found among the dispossessed of his day. As tragically broken as his life eventually became, Jack did, for a period in his life, glimpse the truth that his, and our, personal wholeness is inextricably linked to our connection with all of humanity. In saying "I wished I were a Negro" or "We Mexicans" I think Jack was reaching for that connection. It was a connection that ultimately eluded him. But in his very act of reaching, Kerouac becomes our spirit guide.

For this we say, God bless Jack Kerouac.

CHAPTER THIRTEEN

We Need A Little Beat-ness, Right This Very Moment

On Sunday January 30, 2005, a lengthy, top-of-the-page obituary ran in the *New York Times* for a 79-year-old man named Lucien Carr. The late Mr. Carr had a life long career as a news editor for United Press International, and became a motorcycle and boating enthusiast in his retirement. He was survived by three sons and had a worthy life and career. But how did he rate such a prominent *New York Times* obituary in the year 2005?

Lucien Carr was the catalyst for the initial coming together, "birth of the Beat Generation" meet-ups, on New York City's Upper West Side in the mid-1940s. He introduced Ginsberg, Kerouac, and Burroughs to one another, having known Burroughs from their growing-up days in St. Louis. While he never did any Beat writing himself, and never published any kind of a Beat memoir, Carr was a part of that initial constellation of influential individuals. His obituary included a 1953 photograph of him with Burroughs and Ginsberg.

What struck me the most about Carr's obituary is how a lesser-known figure (compared to Kerouac, Ginsberg, Burroughs, Cassady, et. al.) in the overall Beat movement came to be heralded in the mainstream press as a "Founder and Muse of the Beat Generation," as the *New York Times* headline put it. Although he kept up his contacts with many of his Beat compatriots throughout his life, Carr did not really participate in this movement in the same way as the others. He was more of a networker, and conversational-ist, while the others were writers who put their ideas into print. But what I take from his obituary is one more indicator that the Beats are indeed more prominent, valued, and visible now than in their initial heyday. I'll hazard the guess that had Mr. Carr died in, say, 1960 his death would not have garnered the level of attention that it did when he passed away in 2005. The promi-nence of his obituary was as much a statement about the rebirth of the Beats as it was about the life of Lucien Carr.

Why this rebirth? This book has explored many of my speculations and answers to that question. I suggest that the Beats are striking a contempo-rary spiritual chord with even more resonance than they did in the 1950s and 60s. Let me offer yet another marker, to which I alluded in the opening paragraphs of the previous chapter, as to how the Beat goes on.

In May, 2001, the original 120 foot scroll manuscript of Jack Kerouac's *On the Road* was sold in New York City by the prestigious Christie's Auction House. Part of the legend of the *On the Road* scroll, and which the *Times* dutifully reported in Carr's obituary, was that Lucien Carr provided the paper to Kerouac for his writing marathon. Whatever the story of its origins, the manuscript was purchased for just under two and a half million dollars. According to Christie's auctioneer Francis Wahlgren this figure set "a new world record (paid for) a literary manuscript at auction."

The buyer was Mr. James Irsay of Indianapolis, Indiana. He currently owns the Indianapolis Colts NFL football franchise. He also collects pop cul-tural artifacts of the 1950s, 60s, and 70s, with a particular fancy for guitars once belonging to Jimi Hendrix, Jerry Garcia, and others. To Irsay's blessed and eternal credit he did not put this document in a private collection with his guitars. Instead he has arranged, with understandably strict security and preservation arrangements, for the manuscript to be offered for free and public viewing in a number of locales around the United States and, possibly, around the world.

I attended the opening exhibition of the *On the Road* scroll at Marquette University in Milwaukee, Wisconsin, in September of 2004. Of the one hun-dred or more people who crowded into the exhibition area of a Marquette University library, I was one of maybe two or three other persons in the room who were even alive when *On the Road* was written. (Okay, I was only

THE BEAT FACE OF GOD

six years old). Most of the viewers were in their late teens and early 20s, and they lingered for a long time after the exhibit's opening program just to look through the long glass case and take in the words on a long yellowed strip of paper that had been typed by Jack Kerouac over half a century earlier. His penciled in corrections and additions in the margins are still visible.

When, during a question and answer session, I asked one of the participants in the opening program—who was around my age—why this manuscript, and the book it gave rise to, draws such a large crowd of teens and twenty-somethings, his answer was, "Because people keep having babies!" What I think he meant was that *On the Road* is a classic, coming-of-age novel with enough universality about it to transcend race, gender, religion, sexual orientation, or any of the other categories this culture slices itself into. Sal Paradise's attempt to answer the "Who am I?" question (as related in the previous chapter) is one that any reasonably aware young person confronts as he or she moves into adulthood.

Watching, and talking with, these young people—many of them looking pretty Beat themselves—as they soaked up this document, I was especially struck by the comments of one young man in his late twenties. I interviewed him for an article I was writing about the opening of this exhibit. He said: "I am in awe, man. I am reading the actual manuscript. A couple of years ago there was an exhibit of a DaVinci painting here; and this is like standing in front of a DaVinci. It is like being in the presence of a master." In citing the impact that *On the Road* had on him this gentleman noted, "The first time I ever read Kerouac, that was it. I became an artist, became a painter." A local poet, who was a few decades older than this young man, and who goes by the single name of Antler, had this to say: "Just seeing this represents the promise of endless freedom and the creative spirit. It is an encouragement to writers to give it your all."

The uplift I felt in hearing these, and similar kinds of sentiments at this exhibit, was tempered with a pronounced element of sadness. I felt sad that Jack Kerouac did not live to see the way in which his efforts have inspired future generations of writers, poets, and artists. The ridicule with which both the mainstream literary establishment and the mainstream media treated him was one of the contributing factors in Kerouac's retreat into alcoholism. His heavy drinking from the mid-1960s on was, in effect, a prolonged suicide. Truman Capote's derisive and dismissive commentary on Kerouac's work, "That's not writing, that's typing," was typical of the contempt Kerouac received in his day. It's too bad—in fact it's downright tragic—that Jack did not get the chance to see the effect of his so-called "typing" upon future generations of aspiring writers and artists who seek to give voice and expression to their creative spirit. These thoughts were in my mind as I viewed the *On the Road* scroll, which I consider to be a truly sacred document and artifact.

Why are the Beats bigger now, more than ever? I say it's because we need them now, more than ever. In searching for words to capture why I feel this way I got yet another gift from Kerouac. In a 2004 release of a collection of his personal journal writings from 1947-54 titled *Jack Kerouac—Windblown World*, (Douglas Brinkley, editor) I found a line from a 1948 entry that practically jumped off the page and whacked me up-side the head. Kerouac wrote: "In America there is a *claw* [original emphasis] hanging over our brains, which must be pushed aside else it will clutch and strangle our real selves." If there is a better metaphor than this for the spiritual condition of America in the first decade of this twenty-first century I've yet to come across it. It is especially apt in our post-9/11 state of mind.

Jack wrote these words—a specific date for them is not given—in 1948, in the midst of his travels around America after World War II. This was the same year that twenty-six year old Jack Kerouac, aged 26, and John Clellon Holmes coined the term Beat Generation. Were he still alive, and now in his mid-80s, Kerouac could have written these same words last week and they'd be just as timely.

A "claw hanging over our brains." Burroughs would have liked that; as would have Ginsberg and Michael McClure and numerous others of the "angelheaded hipsters" that Jack had met by then, or would come to meet in later years. For them, and their many kindred spirits, the claw was an increasingly enforced way of living and thinking and being from which little deviation was tolerated. Even in today's comparatively more tolerant atmosphere of diverse thinking and varied life-styles, Kerouac's claw still hangs. This claw may not be as visible or blatant, but it is still there; and it has an impact, I feel, on both our personal and communal lives.

Playing off Kerouac's metaphor, then, I'd like to suggest a pair of claws, or talons, that have got their hooks into our brains right now. They are the claws of consumerism and anti-terrorism. If the relationship between these two "isms" seems tenuous, I offer the reminder that in the aftermath of the September 11, 2001 attacks on the World Trade Center and the Pentagon, President Bush told his fellow citizens that one way to defy the terrorists was…to go shopping. Let's take it one claw at a time.

I do not wish to be self-righteous. I am a consumer who likes my stuff and my creature comforts. So did Kerouac for that matter. The first thing he did when he finally made some decent money from his writing was to buy a nice big house—bigger than the one my wife and I own—in the rather upscale community of Northport, Long Island for himself and his mother. In today's terminology, he moved to the 'burbs. Neither am I against a person being wealthy. If James Irsay had not had two and a half million dollars at his disposal that allowed him to purchase the *On the Road* scroll, I very likely would have been never seen it for myself.

The claw is not our human tendency, or need, for acquisition as such. The damaging hook comes when acquisition becomes a substitute for meaning or authenticity. The claw digs in when acquisition becomes an attempt to fill up a spiritual hole that no amount of things will ever fill up.

Jesus put it far better than I, or most other human beings, when he said, "What does it profit a man if he gains the whole world and loses his soul?" Jesus' words were pretty straightforward. He wasn't making an arcane or obscure point of theology or philosophy when he spoke them. He spoke a simple human truth that transcends the bounds of any one religion or school of philosophy. But we don't listen to him. While few would take issue with Jesus' words, fewer still recognize, much less accept, the truth behind them, despite the fact that the vast majority of Americans call themselves Christians, i.e. followers of Jesus.

Maybe one way to recast Jesus' question would be to reframe it as questions like these: When will you have enough stuff? How much stuff will finally get you to your personal Promised Land? Or, to take it to the societal level: How many more Wal-Marts and shopping malls do we need to build before the American Dream is achieved? And if our President says we can fight terrorism by buying things, how should we respond?

Where is the Beat-ness we need in all this? I don't see the Beats as being anti-materialists so much as I think they had a good understanding as to what materialism could and could not deliver. I go back to one definition of Beat, which is a willingness to be reduced to one's bare essentials, to be willing to strip away the various poses, pretensions, and pretexts we use and instead face the essential questions of "Who am I?" and "Who am I apart from my attachments, my poses, and my things?" One of my favorite passages in all of Jack Kerouac's writings, found in *The Dharma Bums*, plays off this definition as Kerouac brings a truck driver to his own Beat moment.

Kerouac, as his fictional counterpart Ray Smith, is hitchhiking from California to North Carolina to be with his family for Christmas and gets a ride with a truck driver from Ohio. Smith/Kerouac has spent the fall of 1955 in the Bay Area with Japhy Ryder (Gary Snyder), while at the height of Kerouac's Buddhist phase, and now he's heading back East. Somewhere outside of Tucson, Ray and the truck driver stop at a grocery store and pick up a couple of steaks and a quart of milk. They then drive out into the desert, build a fire, and Smith/Kerouac prepares their meal. Here's what follows:

> We had just steak and milk, a great protein feast, squatting there in the sand as highway cars zipped by our little red fire. "Where'd you *learn* to do all these funny things?" he laughed. "And you know I say funny because there's something so durned sensible about 'em. Here I am killin myself drivin this rig back and forth from Ohio to L.A. and I make more money than you ever had in your whole life as a hobo, but you're the one who enjoys life and not only that but you do it without workin or a whole lot of money. Now who's smart, you or me?" And he had a nice home in Ohio with wife, daughter, Christmas tree, two cars, garage, lawn, lawn mower, but he couldn't enjoy any of it because he really wasn't free. It was sadly true. It didn't mean I was a better man than he was, however, he was a great man and I liked him and he liked me...

Kerouac doesn't put down, or look down on, the truck driver for the way he's living; instead he provides him with an experience that puts a crack in his consciousness. The trucker gains a perspective on his life that he did not previously have. And what does Kerouac mean when he says his truck driver friend "really wasn't free."? Kerouac doesn't say. He just leaves the phrase hanging, and then adds the caveat that he doesn't think he's any better than the truck driver for the way he (Kerouac/Smith) has chosen to live, before moving on to other things.

Perhaps Kerouac meant that the driver has allowed himself to become defined both by his possessions—such as they are—and by a way of living that he's never examined in any critical way. Note that Kerouac does not say there's anything *wrong* with the driver having his "two cars, garage, lawn, (and) lawn mower," but that he "couldn't enjoy any of it." Kerouac had just come out of a Buddhist immersion, with a little help from Gary Snyder and Phil Whalen, before making this return trip from the Bay Area. One of the primary Buddhist teachings, as we've already seen, is that the cause of suffering is undue attachment to things we think we want. From this Buddhist perspective Kerouac observed that his trucker friend "really wasn't free." This particular Buddhist principle, by the way, is in basic accord with Jesus' words, which we just saw. The driver gets it, if only for a moment. He may not renounce his way of life, but maybe he's caught a glimpse from Kerouac that the life he lives will not bring him real fulfillment.

Given our current culture's materialistic obsession, what this country needs right now is the same moment of awareness, or shock of recognition, that Kerouac provided his truck driver friend; a Beat Moment, if you will. We need this trucker's crack-in-consciousness experience writ large. We, as a society, are not going to throw our whole way of life overboard, anymore than Kerouac's trucker was going to renounce his way of living. But we could seriously ask ourselves an expanded version of the question Jesus posed: "What does it profit a nation if it gains the lion's share of the world's wealth and loses its soul?" Unless and until we are willing to seriously face that question a materialistic claw will remain affixed to our brains. Unless and until we do that we will continue to be the recipients, deserved or not, of the enmity of a good deal of the rest of the world—particularly the non-wealthy western nations and third world nations. This gets us to the second claw.

Let me share an experience: In the summer of 2002 I was in Quebec City attending a conference of the Unitarian Universalists. I broke away from the conference proceedings one evening to have dinner with a friend who lives in the adjourning city of Ste. Foy, and who had been a great help to me in writing my previous book *Kerouac's Nashua Connection*. His name is Jacques Kirouac. He is a good, decent, generous, and kind man. He bears absolutely no ill will towards the United States or its citizens. We were, at the time, less than a year removed from the 9/11 attacks, and at some point we talked about them.

English is not Jacques' original language. But since his English is far better than my French our conversation was in English. Jacques reached for words he hoped would accurately convey his feelings as he expressed to me the shock and horror he felt as the terrorist attacks took place. He reached for words he hoped would convey his deep remorse over the Americans who perished on that horrific day. It seemed he needed to say these things to an American, and I was providing him an opportunity to do so. Then he struggled even harder, to the point of stretching his hands out into the air as if he were trying to pull in the right words from somewhere beyond him: "But... Steve...do you know...do you see...you are so rich...you are so powerful...?" That was as much as he could do. His English failed him, though I doubt that any more fluency on his part would have helped. He'd said all that could be said. And all I could do was nod and say, "Yes, I know...I see..." Our conversation then moved on to other things.

Personally, I am neither rich nor powerful, and my French-Canadian friend knew that. What he was trying to convey to me had to do with the image my country projects, in large measure, to the world at large. We *do* look like a nation that has gained much of the world while losing much of its soul. But our minds will never be open enough to seriously examine that image and its implications, and how to respond to it, so long as that second claw of anti-terrorism remains embedded in our brains. Before pursuing this point further, however, we need to back up a bit for some historical perspective.

In 1948, and the years that followed, a similar claw that bears an uncanny resemblance to this claw of anti-terrorism gripped our societal mind—anti-Communism. To be sure, in the aftermath of the Second World War, there were Communists who seriously sought the downfall of America. Nikita Khrushchev, Premier of the Soviet Union during much of the 1950s did say, in referring to the United States, "We will bury you." Whether he was alluding to military conquest is highly questionable, but his words were taken seriously. And indeed today, there are terrorists in this world who wish to do us great harm, and have in fact done so. But in labeling blacklisted writers, and creating the McCarthy era hearings that destroyed lives and careers, our fear of communism did far greater harm to our national soul and psyche, and to our overall well-being as a nation, than anything the Communists themselves ever did. Our fear of terrorism, as incited and prolonged by the federal government is now doing the same damage to us.

One of the more pronounced expressions of our fear of Communism in the 1950s and early 60s—although scarcely acknowledged as such—was an intense religiosity in which the will of the Christian God was more or less equated with the role America was playing in the world in the post-War era. The so-called American Way of Life, and God's plan for humanity became essentially synonymous. This melding of nationalism and religion, which was primarily of the conservative Christian variety, as there was precious little other, clamped its claw onto our collective cultural consciousness. Given this meld, it made a certain kind of sense for Francis Cardinal Spellman—one of the most powerful religious figures in America of his day—to call the first large contingent of young Americans sent, willingly or not, to fight in Vietnam, "soldiers of Christ."

Most of our obedient citizens would not have called this religiosity an expression or outgrowth of fear, but that, in good measure, is what it was. After all, there is no better way to assuage one's fear of an enemy, real or imagined, than to become as convinced as you can that God is on your side. In addition, any challenge to this collective cultural consciousness was seen as truly subversive. This perceived subversion led FBI Director, J. Edgar Hoover, to deliver his previously noted warning to the Republican National Convention in 1960, that the three major enemies of America were "communists, eggheads, and beatniks." It was a warning that resonated well with the populace at large.

Beatniks? In conventional American culture, the evils of "godless Communism" were a given, of course. At the time the adjective and the noun constituted one word: godlesscommunism. And a suspicion of the patriotism and loyalty of intellectuals and academicians (i.e. "eggheads") has long been a standard fare of the political and cultural right wing in this country. But how did the beatniks get to be the third member of Mr. Hoover's trinity of subversion? The Beats had no clearly defined political agenda of any sort. Allen Ginsberg's flirtation with the New Left was about the closest they ever came, and that didn't happen until the Beat era was pretty well over.

What really rankled the likes of J. Edgar Hoover, along with his millions of followers and admirers across the land, was the Beats' refusal to unquestioningly and uncritically buy into the melding of God and Country. The Beats were no more anti-American than they were anti-materialist, but they were not willing to conform to someone else's definition of what a good American was. This was especially so when that Someone Else was an overarching cultural mentality whose claw, as Kerouac clearly saw, was hovering over the brains of rank and file Americans, the great majority of whom were good and decent human beings, like my fine parents.

In the cultural and political milieu of the America of the 1950s and early 60s the Beats represented the free and creative spirit, or the Life Force, that percolates below the surface—with its occasional spill-overs—of practically any civilization. Such a spirit is generally feared more than it is embraced. The poem is far more powerful than the political manifesto as Ginsberg, McClure, Corso, Ferlinghetti, Snyder, Lamantia, di Prima, and a host of others well knew. In totalitarian regimes, in fact, poets have been arrested, jailed for life, and exiled or executed for writing poems. While not primarily a poet, Kerouac gave voice to the exuberance of the creative spirit, along with its accompanying undertone of sadness and tragedy, in *On the Road*, and in his follow-up work, *The Dharma Bums*. And that voice reached the ears, and the minds, of a host of those who had been asking themselves, "Am I the only one out here who feels this way?"

Kerouac didn't even intend to generate a counter-cultural force or movement. He was baffled, in fact, by all that came flying out of the bottle he uncorked. In *On the Road* he just wanted to tell a story about his crazed, mystical, and mystifying companion of the road, whom he called Dean Moriarty. But, wittingly or not Kerouac made Neal Cassady/Dean Moriarty the embodiment of the unbounded Life Force; and the energy of his book energized, in turn, a whole generation.

Fast forward now nearly five decades. The claw of anti-Communism has become recast as the claw of anti-terrorism, and the same kind of nationalistic religiosity that accompanied the former now undergirds the latter. Once again, for political purposes by our government, God has become an American. Just as "godlesscommunist" became a single word in the 1950s, so, in this day, has "islamicterrorist." The sacred icon of this nationalistic religiosity is the magnetic yellow ribbon. In fact, what better symbol could there be for the combined claws of anti-terrorism and consumerism than a yellow ribbon stuck to the back of a gas guzzling behemoth? Along with this symbol, sold for ten dollars to thousands of consumers, the dogma of this religiosity is expressed in such creedal formulations as "Support the troops" or "God bless America."

I've yet to meet anyone, whatever his/her political philosophy, or opinion on the Iraqi War, who does not support the troops, in the sense of caring for the wellbeing of the individuals who serve. Members of my own congregation have joined the military and gone off to war since 9/11; how can I not support them? So far, blessedly, I have not had to officiate any of their funerals. My issue, in fact, is neither with yellow ribbons nor exhortations to support the troops. Symbols and slogans do indeed have their valid and legitimate place in human affairs and dealings. Idolatry occurs when any symbol—be it a yellow ribbon or anything else—becomes an impediment to honest inquiry into the rightness, and the wisdom, of our invading a foreign country, however heinous its Head of State may have been. My issue instead is with idolatry.

Idolatry occurs when a slogan like "God bless America" morphs into a dogma that becomes a firewall against any kind of critical thought as to how our standing and image, deserved or not, in the world community made us the target of terrorists in the first place. It is this kind of idolatry that also opens the way for the acceptance of practices not generally tolerated in a supposedly free, open, and democratic society. This kind of idolatry leads to the cultural condition Kerouac described so well nearly 60 years ago as a young man in the process of discovering his native land: "In America there's a *claw* hanging over our brains, which must be pushed aside else it will clutch and strangle our real selves."

In the face of idolatry it is absolutely crucial to maintain one's spiritual balance, and cultivate one's spiritual nurture and well-being. This, I believe, is what the Beats were trying to do in their day. As I've already suggested, they were neither anti-materialist nor anti-American; but they were seeking a spirituality that transcended the idolatries of materialism and nationalism. As with any search for our real selves, or journey of the spirit, some of the roads taken are healthier, and more fruitful, than others. Some, tragically, even lead to personal destruction. In this latter regard, one of the saddest, and yet curiously soulful, chapters in all of Beat lore is Kerouac's book *Big Sur*, which foreshadows the beginning of the end for Jack. But the Beats had the courage to walk their roads, and we need the legacy of their journey-making today more than ever.

The spiritual journey is one that often begins with a sense of alienation or isolation and reaches for connection. As Paul Tillich explained it, we reach out from alienation in search of a relationship with That Which Is Greater Than Ourselves, however such may be named. And the spiritual is not pursued and nurtured in isolation from the social, cultural, and political realms, or larger life context, within which the seeker lives and moves. In addition, one cannot feel alienated from something unless s/he also, ultimately, wishes to bond with it. The flip side of alienation is a yearning and a reaching for attachment, for a spiritual bond. You cannot be a true "mis-fit" without also seeking for a "fit."

The claws I've been describing over the course of this chapter have left me with a greater sense of alienation, and with a greater sense of being a mis-fit in my own land, than at any time I can recall in my 60 years of living—including the tumultuous years of the late 1960s when I entered adulthood. A person in such a predicament as mine has basically two choices: Retreat into nihilism, or find a spiritual stance that will keep you meaningfully engaged with the very thing from which you also feel separated and alienated. Having never found nihilism all that attractive, I opt for engaged spirituality. In pursuing this spirituality, I have turned to the Beats, flawed, and sometimes even flakey, human beings that they were. They are my spirit guides.

Part of the spiritual journey involves cultivating what Kerouac called a "Beatific" life, a life that lives out one's spiritual connection to others, and to all of life, through simple deeds and acts of kindness and compassion. Kerouac looked to the Beatitudes of Jesus, as spoken in the Sermon on the Mount, as pointing to this aspect of Beat-ness. Beatitude involves cultivating a sense of empathy with the life that surrounds us. When, during his appearance on the Steve Allen Show in the fall of 1959, Kerouac was asked by Mr. Allen to define Beat, he had a one-word answer, "Well...sympathetic." I believe what he meant there was that Beat, as Beatific, indicated having a sense of deep identification with Life Itself, and with those whom Jesus termed "the least of these."

The Beats also sought a spiritual bond with this land that transcended the political maneuverings of those who supposedly "rule" it. This is a bond I seek for myself; now more than ever. It is the bond Jack Kerouac wrote of as he "sat on the broken down river pier watching the long, long skies over New Jersey and sense(d) all that raw land that rolls in one unbelievable huge bulge over to the West Coast, and all that road going, all the people dreaming in the immensity of it..." A land where the "evening star must be drooping and shedding her sparkler dims on the prairie, which is just before the coming of the complete night that blesses the earth, darkens all rivers, cups the peaks, and folds the final shore in..." For my money, that passage stands up to anything that can be found in all of American literature when it comes to just plain damned good writing! And it stands because it was written out of Jack Kerouac's love for this land; a love that transcended the claws of his day, and those of ours today.

Like Woody Guthrie, whom I consider to be one of the spiritual forerunners of the Beats, Jack Kerouac also knew that "This land was made for you and me..." The original title of Woody's signature song, by the way, was "God Blessed America for Me," and was originally written as a response to Irving Berlin's "God Bless America." This land of ours—like the earth itself—was made for those who still seek and sense its eternal rhythms, even as its earliest human inhabitants did. This land was made for those who still listen for its beat, and who still believe there is something there to hear. This is the beat that the Beats themselves sought to give voice to in their writing.

In 1955 Allen Ginsberg concluded his caustic, biting, sarcastic, and bombastic poem *America* with the words, "America, I'm putting my queer shoulder to the wheel." Even with all that preceded that line, Allen must have sensed something worthy in this land, which feared his sexual orientation then even more than it does today. Ginsberg sought a bond somewhere beyond the madness that he saw destroying "the best minds of my generation." So he wrote poetry, in order that he could breathe; and in so doing brought a breath of life to countless others. His pursuit of the Buddhist path also brought Ginsberg to an understanding of that connection between Beat and Beatific.

We live in a maze as we seek to find our ways through a land that both is and is not ours; and through a universe which we feel both estranged from and at One with. Our place in this maze is always changing. Sometimes our journey within it takes us through a strange and alien land, and sometimes it brings us home. We each have to find our own way of navigating this maze of the spirit. We each have to put a shoulder, queer or not, to the wheel. And in so doing, we look to those who would guide us. My spirit guides were, and are, the holy misfits. These holy misfits were also called The Beats.

ISBN 1-41205374-9